Referential Communication Tasks

Second Language Research:
Theoretical and Methodological Issues
Susan Gass and Jacquelyn Schachter, Editors

Tarone/Gass/Cohen ● Research Methodology in
Second-Language Acquisition

Schachter/Gass ● Second Language
Classroom Research:
Issues and Opportunities

Gass ● Input, Interaction, and the
Second Language Learner

Monographs on Research Methodology

Yule ● Referential
Communication Tasks

Referential Communication Tasks

George Yule

LEA LAWRENCE ERLBAUM ASSOCIATES, PUBLISHERS
1997 Mahwah, New Jersey

Lawrence Erlbaum Associates, Inc., Publishers
10 Industrial Avenue
Mahwah, New Jersey 07430

Cover design by Kathryn Houghtaling

Library of Congress Cataloging-in-Publication Data

Yule, George.
Referential communication tasks / George Yule.
       p. cm.
   Includes bibliographical references (p. 89) and
index.
     ISBN 0-8058-2003-5 (alk. paper). — ISBN 0-
8058-2004-3 (pbk : alk. paper)
     1. Language acquisition—Research—Methodol-
ogy. 2. Reference (Linguistics) I. Title.
    P118.Y85   1997
    401'.93'072—dc21   96–52269
                                             CIP

Printed in the United States of America
10 9 8 7 6 5 4 3 2 1

Contents

Foreword

This series is born of our belief that to adequately understand conclusions drawn from second language acquisition research, one must understand the methodology that is used to elicit data for that research. The concern with research methodology is common in all fields, but it takes on particular significance in second language research given the interdisciplinary nature of the field and the varying perspectives of second language researchers. Within a single common field, we have psychologists talking to linguists; we have sociolinguists concerned with variation talking to sociolinguists concerned with pragmatics; we have ethnographers talking to generative grammarians. Although all of this is healthy for the long-term outcome of the field, it is problematic in that researchers bring with them research traditions from their own disciplines. Again, this is ultimately healthy, but can lead to serious misunderstandings, in the short term, of the value of a particular elicitation instrument. As a result, research traditions are "attacked" through their methodologies without a full understanding of what linguistic/psycholinguistic/sociolinguistic knowledge or abilities a particular instrument is intended to tap. This series of monographs is an attempt to bring to light just these issues.

The series consists of monographs, each devoted to a particular data-collection method or instrument. Each monograph probes a specific research method or tool, discussing the history of the instrument as well as its current uses. A major feature of each monograph is an exploration of what the research instrument does and does not purport to tell us about second language acquisition or use. Each monograph addresses the kinds of research questions for which the method or instrument is best suited, its underlying assumptions, a characterization of the method or instrument, and an extended description of its use, including problems associated with its use. It is hoped that the series as a whole will reflect the state of the "research" art in second language acquisition. It is only through a deeper understanding of the strengths and weaknesses, and the advantages and disadvantages of particular research tools, that the field of second language acquisition can get beyond issues of methodology and begin to work together as a collective whole.

—Susan Gass
—Jacquelyn Schachter
Series Editors

Acknowledgments

This book has its origins in research projects, initiated almost 20 years ago, that would not have been possible without the innovative thinking and intellectual energy of Gillian Brown at Edinburgh University. There would have been less depth and less relevance for the field of second language acquisition if I had not been guided by the insights and enthusiasm of Elaine Tarone at the University of Minnesota. And the work would not have been written without the advice, support, and encouragement of Maryann Overstreet at the University of Hawaii. To these three generous women, many thanks. Many others, both colleagues and students, have contributed over the years to the discussion presented in these pages. I particularly acknowledge the contributions of Hugh Buckingham, Elin Epperson, Wayne Gregory, Doris Macdonald, and Maggie Powers, while we were all at Louisiana State University. I also thank the community of the ESL Department at the University of Hawai'i at Manoa, particularly Craig Chaudron and Ricky Jacobs, for their support while, as a visiting colleague, I was writing this book. To all, mahalo nui loa.

1

Overview

Referential communication is the term given to communicative acts, generally spoken, in which some kind of information is exchanged between two speakers. This information exchange is typically dependent on successful acts of reference, whereby entities (human and nonhuman) are identified (by naming or describing), are located or moved relative to other entities (by giving instructions or directions), or are followed through sequences of locations and events (by recounting an incident or a narrative). In one established definition, referential communication is described as: "that type of communication involved in such activities as giving directions on a map, telling someone how to assemble a piece of equipment, or how to select a specific object from a larger set of objects" (Dickson, 1982, p. 1).

What are presented in this definition as *activities* are examples of what, in the area of second language studies, are more typically described as *tasks*. They might be real-world tasks encountered in everyday experience or pedagogical tasks specifically designed for second language classroom use. When the notion of task is reviewed in studies of second language teaching, one common concept can be identified in the definitions: "they all imply that tasks involve communicative language use in which the user's attention is focused on meaning rather than linguistic structure" (Nunan, 1989, p. 10).

This focus on meaning rather than structure tends to be matched by a general interest in the function of utterances rather than their form and a concern with the nature of actual communicative performance on a particular occasion rather than with the analysis of linguistic competence at some abstract level.

Described in this way, referential communication tasks represent research instruments that differ in many ways from others more usually employed in the investigation of second language acquisition. In order to appreciate that difference, some brief background information has to be considered.

BACKGROUND

What is now known as referential communication can be traced back to ideas presented by Piaget during the 1920s in connection with his studies of children's development. Focusing specifically on the development of verbal abilities in children, Piaget drew attention to a noticeable shift away from *egocentric speech* that occurred around 6 or 7 years of age. The tasks devised to explore this phenomenon (cf. Piaget, 1959; Piaget & Inhelder, 1956) required the children to communicate information in such a way that their ability to adapt the message to another's perspective could be analyzed. Although he did not label them as such, Piaget was using referential communication tasks.

However, it was not until the 1960s that a more active research field exploring referential communication emerged. During that period, it became apparent to researchers that the concept of egocentric speech (i.e., communication not adapted to the listener) had much more complexity than the single cognitive construct offered by Piaget. The range of factors found to be capable of influencing children's communicative performance increased substantially. Theoretically different explanations for observed behavior were explored (e.g., Vygotsky, 1962) and the idea of *role-taking* was investigated in much greater depth (e.g., Flavell, Botkin, Fry, Wright, & Jarvis, 1968). For many investigators, referential communication ceased to be primarily a psychological concept and was increasingly interpreted from the perspective of social knowledge. For two of the most influential researchers at the time, the crucial distinction was characterized in terms of "social versus non-social speech" (Glucksberg & Krauss, 1967). Social speech is edited communication, produced specifically to take account of some other (the current listener) and responsive to what the other does, knows, and says. Nonsocial speech is unedited, produced as an expression of the perspective of self (the speaker only), and not responsive to what the other does, knows, or says. Social speech appears to develop after nonsocial speech. Related to this social–interactional perspective, there was the clear realization that utterances never "exhaust the potential features" (Olson, 1970, p. 264) of a referent, but specify only certain features. It followed that variation in the selection of relevant features would necessarily be an inherent aspect of referential communication.

It was also during this period that the distinction between linguistic competence and communicative competence (Hymes, 1971) began to attract more interest among those studying language. In a related development, a clearer distinction was drawn between the general development of verbal ability and the notion of *communicative effectiveness* as something that could be found in performance to a greater or lesser extent. Proposing that there is such a thing as the ability to distinguish between potentially effective versus ineffective messages inevitably leads to a consideration of some message-analytic capacity (cf. Asher, 1976). In essence, this is metacommunicative ability, or communicating about communicating. In one of its simplest manifestations, this would be one function of feedback in a task where difficulty in understanding the message is indicated. Having the ability to use feedback to make revisions to a message or, more generally, to conceive of messages as potential objects of analysis, may have been what distinguished the older from younger children in some of Piaget's original explorations. If feedback, or even anticipated feedback, can influence the message being communicated, then once again variation in the selection of the message will be an unavoidable aspect of communicative acts. In one of the major reviews of this era of research, Asher (1979) provided the following summary: "Communication effectiveness involves a number of separate skills whose relevance to performance varies as a function of the nature of the listener and the nature of the task" (p. 194).

We return, throughout this book, to many of these issues regarding the nature of communicative effectiveness, the role of feedback, the impact of social knowledge, and the overwhelming fact of variation in message form. However, it is worth noting that all this research on the development of referential communication skills among children is almost totally ignored (then and now) in reviews of what is called *first language* (L1) *acquisition.* Something else entirely has been absorbing most investigators of L1 acquisition and it has largely dominated the basic research agenda in *second language* (L2) *acquisition* studies, too.

Structure Versus Function

In most reviews of L1 and L2 acquisition research, the spotlight has been on morphology and syntax. In answer to the question, "what is being acquired?" the L2 acquisition field has traditionally pointed to grammatical morphemes (e.g., words containing the inflections *-ing* or *-s*) and grammatical structures (e.g., sentences containing negative or question forms and word orders). The early dominance of this perspective is apparent in the focus of most of the papers collected in Hatch (1978a). As the theoretical concepts and the forms being investigated have become more complex, the concern with morpho-syntax has not diminished. From the "natural order" of English morphemes at the core of Krashen's Monitor Theory (cf. Krashen & Terrell, 1983) to the "developmental sequence" of word order rules at the heart of Pienemann's Teachability Hypothesis (cf. Pienemann & Johnston, 1987), the dominant concept for most research has been how L2 morpho-syntactic forms are acquired.

Referential communication tasks are not particularly useful instruments for addressing morpho-syntactic development as typically conceived, largely because they do not guarantee obligatory contexts for the occurrence of specific morpho-syntactic forms (cf. Gass, Cohen, & Tarone, 1994; Mackey, 1994; Pienemann, Johnston, & Brindley, 1988). They can yield insights into the use of grammatical structures, but only within the larger activity of speakers making sense of each other (i.e., being focused on meaning). From a linguistic perspective, referential communication tasks appear to be more concerned with semantics (particularly with regard to vocabulary) and pragmatics (speaker meaning in context) than with morpho-syntax. Support for a fundamental difference can be found in Zurif's (1990) proposal that there must be "a neurological distinction between, on the one hand, a system supporting reference (one that is likely embedded in, and structured by, our knowledge about objects in the world) and, on the other hand, a uniquely linguistic system for the representation of grammatical knowledge" (p. 181). Given this wider perspective, tasks involving referential communication will also be concerned with issues in psychology, such as the nature of mental representations and processes, as well as social concerns that arise from the nature of face-to-face interaction. With these rather special characteristics, research undertaken via these tasks will tend to be distinguished from other L2 research and theoretical perspectives along a number of dimensions.

The major tradition influencing many L2 acquisition researchers has continued to be structuralist in orientation. For the minority who have been interested in it, referential communication has had a strongly functionalist character. In an attempt to illustrate some of the major differences between a structurally oriented perspective and one more attracted to a functionalist view, the following differences are listed as representative, not of two people or even of two extreme groups, but of two divergent tendencies noticeable in assumptions of what is important and hence worthy of research energy. These differences are summarized in Table 1.1.

Instead of narrowly focusing on linguistic form (e.g., morphology), those who use referential communication tasks tend to be concerned with pragmatic functions (e.g., acts of reference). Instead of absolute correctness or accuracy of form, it is relative success or effectiveness of the referential act that is considered. Rather than rule-based adherence (or not) being judged, relative level of appropriateness to situation is assessed. Instead of a single unifying abstract construct called *competence* as the object of study, the variable manifestations of actual performance are recorded and analyzed. Instead of *stages* of acquisition, mechanically following one after the other, there are

TABLE 1.1

Focus of Referential Communication Research
Versus Traditional L2 Acquisition Research

L2 acquisition	Referential communication
Linguistic form	Pragmatic function
(e.g., morphology)	(e.g., acts of reference)
Accuracy of form	Effectiveness of act
Adherence to rules	Situational appropriateness
Abstract competence	Situated performance
Acquisition stages	Developmental changes
(mechanical)	(organic)
Nativist explanations	Experiential explanations
Uniformity sought	Variation explored
Failure to acquire	Development of ability
(native-like L2)	(non-native L2)

developmental changes viewed as occurring, organically and
variably, as a result of experience. Rather than nativist concepts
such as innate properties or biological specialization as explanations, there are experiential and social explanations. Instead of a
search for uniformity in the evidence of acquisition, there is an
exploration of variation. And finally, instead of viewing the
large-scale failure to acquire nativelike L2 ability as the thing to
be accounted for (theoretically), the large-scale development of
varying degrees of nonnative communicative ability is treated as
a valid object of investigation.

Methodology

Given these distinct characteristics, it is to be expected that
referential communication research will have looser, or less
tightly controlled, elicitation devices than research that is more
structural in orientation. The analytic frameworks employed
will also be more open and depend on consistency of interpretation rather than on some correct–incorrect dichotomy based
on suppliance of a particular linguistic form. The relevant data
will tend to be the discourse or the interaction, and not the word

or sentence. It will also typically be production data, created by the participating speakers, and not reaction data where choices have been created by the researcher. In many ways, referential communication research will fail to meet many of the criteria traditionally considered crucial for rigorous research methodology. There is unlikely to be sufficient control, nor will the findings be considered technically reliable or easily replicable or even widely generalizable. These criteria, however, are largely a reflection of a structuralist perspective and so it should not be surprising that a shift in perspective would result in a change of criteria for conducting and evaluating the research. Consequently, in the course of the following chapters, a wide range of methodological issues is discussed and the value of different types of elicitation materials is considered. Very much tied to these issues is the typical goal of such research and its relevant context.

CONTEXT AND ROLE

There is no reason, in principle, why referential communication tasks could not be used in informal contexts with natural L2 acquirers. However, in practice, virtually all the research has been conducted in formal contexts such as schools and colleges, and the impetus for most of the research has been related to instructional issues. In L1 research, the focus has been on finding ways to create conditions under which young children (4- to 8-year-olds) can become more effective communicators in a language whose morpho-syntax they have, to a large extent, demonstrably acquired already. In L2 research, the focus has been on attempting to discover the conditions under which adult users of a second language, whose morpho-syntax they have demonstrably not fully acquired already, can manipulate their available linguistic resources to produce task-related, communicatively effective messages.

The contexts of the L2 research have been instructional environments. The goal of most of the research has been the improvement of L2 instructional materials and practices. There should be no illusion that we are exploring any natural acquisition of some communicative capacity. We are looking at the kind of institutionally (and hence, socially) determined concept of mature or well-developed, "on-task," verbal behaviors that are communicatively better than others. The sociocultural concept of *better* in communicative terms is clearly tied to effective task completion in the immediate context. As Long (1985) argued, specifically focusing on pedagogic tasks, "success on these is judged by task accomplishment, not target-like linguistic production" (p. 95).

Recognizing this sociocultural bias is extremely important. Much of the research in referential communication has underlying assumptions concerning the requirements of language in use. The concept of a *target* is not a target language, but what Breen and Candlin (1980) called a *target repertoire*, or the ability to use the L2 in communicative exchanges. Once we expand our perspective from the L2 as simply words and sentences, we are immediately confronted with the existence of sociocultural values. Learning to use an L2 includes developing an awareness of how L2 messages (not structures) are expected to be formed and expressed within communicative events. Some kind of socialization has to take place with respect to community (e.g., classroom) norms of participation. Some kind of social persona has to be assumed and social values have to be recognized.

In its most obvious manifestation, the social persona is the *role* assigned to (or adopted by) a participant in any referential communication task. That role may simply be labeled *the sender* (of information) to *the listener*, but it may also have other subtle dimensions, such as *expert, female gender, higher status individual, non-familiar, proficient speaker,* and many others. The social values to be recognized may be characteristics of *effective talk,* such as brevity, clarity, involvement, good recipient design, and others, that are considered important by a particular group, but may, in fact, reflect a strong cultural bias not shared by many participants in the research (cf. Hall, 1995). As a simple example, Hinds (1987) drew attention to a basic distinction between American and Asian concepts of communicative responsibility. The general monolingual English-language-using culture of the

United States appears to assume that it is the speaker (writer) who bears most responsibility for the success (or not) of a communicative exchange, whereas, for other cultures, particularly those of Asia, much more of that responsibility rests with the listener (reader). Clearly such a large-scale cultural difference will have a profound effect on the relationship between the said and the unsaid in any communicative event.

Having mentioned a number of issues that will necessarily find their way into a discussion of this type of research, we should also devote some attention to the major concepts involved in the type of research instrument under analysis. We must spell out some assumptions concerning the act of reference and the limited nature of the kind of communication we are exploring.

REFERENCE

In order to make sense of referential communication, it is crucial to understand how reference actually works, rather than how we often casually assume it works. It is tempting to think of reference as some kind of basic connection between words and things. It can appear as if there are discrete objects in the world and our language provides discrete labels for each of those objects, or perhaps for each kind of object. In L2 learning, we make blatant use of this assumption when we look in a dictionary for an L2 translation equivalent to the L1 label. As most L2 learners soon discover, this assumption is extremely problematic. There is, in fact, no direct connection between words and things. Words do have a conventional range of reference, but, by themselves, words do not refer. It is people who refer. It is useful to keep in mind that reference is an action through which a speaker (or writer) uses linguistic forms to enable a listener (or reader) to identify something (cf. Lyons, 1977).

For acts of reference to be successful, the listener has to infer correctly which entity the speaker intends to identify by using a particular linguistic expression. When you go out with a group to a restaurant and a waiter asks, "Is your table ready to order?" you tend not to be puzzled by the use of the word *table* in this way. Yet, taking a literal view of reference, a table is a piece of furniture and it cannot be expected to talk. Nor does a piece of furniture normally order food. However, instead of being puzzled, you easily make the conventional inference that the intended referents are the people seated at the table. The key ingredients, then, are a basic *intention to identify*, a *recognition of intention*, and an assumption of collaboration between the participants. It is the trivial, everyday success of that collaboration among members of a social community, sharing a common language, that leads to the assumption that there is a conventional association of certain linguistic expressions with certain types of entities. When this process is represented in a simple way, we can create vocabulary lists from the frequently observed conventional associations and provide those to L2 learners as a kind of shortcut to acquiring referential ability. The typical effect is one in which learners become familiar with the use of each L2 expression as having an extremely limited and fixed range of reference. With only this basis, L2 learners will tend not to develop the kind of collaborative referential patterns of behavior expected by those who use these expressions with the assumption of a wider and more open range of reference.

That assumption is typically based on the experience of linguistic expressions being polysemous (i.e., having multiple related meanings). However, those multiple meanings do not appear to be learned, one by one, for each expression. Rather, the general experience of having to refer to entities for which a conventional label is not known, or from a perspective not previously taken on a particular entity, leads most language users, in their L1, to manipulate available linguistic resources to accomplish the immediate referential goal. In English, they often make use of forms that have a virtually unlimited range of reference (e.g., *thing, stuff*) and modifiers that have local salience (e.g., *red, sticky*). They have expressions that approximate (*a kind of X, a sort of Y*) or work by analogy (*an X or something like that*). They can categorize, on some locally agreed-on, often temporary basis, the entities to which they need to refer, without ever needing to consider the existence of some special, technical, or dictionary terms, as illustrated in the following fragment of dialogue, spoken in connection with replacing some window screens:

A: The part that broke is a little plastic thing, sort of like a wing that turns all the way round.

B: Do we have any more of those wings?

B's question is not about anything that birds and airplanes have.

It is exactly this manipulative, temporary, ad hoc use of language that referential communication tasks are designed to foster. In many cases, the tasks include elements for which no conventional referential labels appear to exist and for which the participants will have to develop, collaboratively, a shared means of identification. We look at many such tasks and how to use them, and consider the different ways that participants' referring expressions might be analyzed.

In the course of earlier studies with young children, researchers focused on two types of referential demands on the speaker's developing ability. One type is essentially an identification-of-referent demand, sometimes viewed as the stochastic dimension (cf. Higgins, Fondocaro, & McCann, 1981; Rosenberg & Cohen, 1966). In a simple task involving the identification of an object (the referent), as distinct from any others (nonreferents), the speaker must have the following three abilities: (a) perceptual ability: to notice specific attributes of referents and nonreferents; (b) comparison ability: to identify critical differences or similarities among those attributes; and (c) linguistic ability: to encode those critical differences.

Although L2 researchers may tend to focus on linguistic ability among these three, it is worth noting what has been observed with regard to comparison ability with L1 children. Younger children (5 years old) generally appear to have this skill, but do not use it unless specifically prompted, asked, or even trained to do so (Whitehurst & Sonnenschein, 1981). They know how, but not when. It is worth keeping this in mind because there is evidence that having such a skill (knowing how) does not automatically mean it is activated when required. Recognizing when to use the skill is a distinct type of knowledge.

The other type of demand is the more familiar role-taking dimension (cf. Flavell et al., 1968; Shantz, 1981), requiring the speaker to take account of the role of the communicative partner. In doing so, the speaker must be able to (a) recognize that the other's perspective must be considered, (b) make reasonably accurate inferences about the other's perspective, (c) use those inferences to edit the developing message, and (d) continually monitor the other and attend to any feedback.

These are demands that are related to the process of getting the information across. They all assume that the other is present, has an identifiable perspective, and can provide feedback. In many of their past experimental uses, referential communication tasks may not always have incorporated these components in a clear way.

COMMUNICATION

The basic view of communication that lies at the heart of all work on referential communication is an information transmission model that dates back to the work of Shannon and Weaver (1949). Although it does not retain the mathematical perspective of the original source, the general information transmission model (cf. Cherry, 1966) continues to make use of concepts such as sender–receiver and message encoding–decoding. It is clearly concerned with the communication of information, particularly factual or propositional information, and what Brown and Yule (1983) described as the transactional function of language. Primarily transactional language is message oriented, and the receiver is expected to understand clearly what was in the message. It is distinguished from primarily interactional language, which Brown and Yule (1983) described as listener oriented, and which includes chat and other types of casual talk where the content of the conversation can be relatively nonspecific. It is important to emphasize that although transactional talk is focused on information and content, it does not exclude information exchange, where two or more participants contribute messages to the transaction. The defining element is the primary focus on message content.

The demands of transactional talk are quite distinct from those normally experienced in casual conversation, as Deese (1974) observed some years ago:

> The correspondence between the ideas possessed by two individuals who are in communication on a common topic is rather poor, a condition which we ordinarily do not notice because we seldom make explicit attempts to validate a communicated idea against the original. When we do, as in the case of giving directions to someone about how to do something, we are suddenly made aware of the discrepancy that exists between "the same" idea in the minds of two different people. Ordinary situations demand that we place only the loosest of interpretations upon some linguistic utterance we hear. (p. 72)

In the case of giving directions, as mentioned here, we are inevitably involved in transactional talk.

Interpersonal Communication

In contrast to transactional talk, interactional talk is typically interpersonally oriented and tied to the maintenance of social relations. This too is communication, but it is not inherently referential communication. We might also note here that there are many other aspects of communication, particularly those associated with work in cross-cultural and interlanguage pragmatics, that are not typically referential (cf. Blum-Kulka, House, & Kasper, 1989; Kasper & Blum-Kulka, 1993). Social interaction in familiar encounters may contain elements that are referential, but the overall sense is one of interpersonal communication where the focus is on the person more than the message. This type of communication is much more fundamental, is acquired early in the L1, and is essential to the social life of individuals in a particular social community (cf. Gallaway & Richards, 1994).

In many ways, this type of communication is characterized by what is not overtly articulated (yet understood) because it is used in contexts where assumptions of shared knowledge are strongest. It is the type of interactive talk most studied by sociologists and cultural anthropologists who are interested in the underlying norms and conventions of everyday life in social communities (cf. Atkinson & Heritage, 1984; Garfinkel, 1967; Gumperz, 1982a). Such talk typically assumes a "reciprocity of perspectives" (Schütz, 1962, p. 10) arising from shared experiences of the world, or proceeds as if that reciprocity does exist even on occasions when it might not (cf. Cicourel, 1974). This type of interpersonal talk represents closeness and familiarity, and is characterized by markers such as *you know (what I mean)*, *and stuff (like that)*, and other expressions that indicate that the speaker does not have to spell out the message content explicitly (cf. Overstreet & Yule, 1997; Schiffrin, 1987). In this respect, interpersonal talk is at the opposite end of the explicitness continuum from referential communication.

Referential Communication

As already emphasized, referential communication is primarily about information transfer or exchange. It is not acquired early in the L1 and, as discussed in chapter 2, may not be fully acquired at all by some individuals as a comfortable function in their first language. It is, however, clearly tied to institutional demands, beginning in school, for decontextualized language use, where the participants are not depending on substantially shared experiences or common knowledge. It requires decentering, or the recognition that others typically do not already know or see what the self obviously does. It is, in spoken language, the necessary transition type of communicative language use that leads to literacy and the ability to cope with written language communication. Just as most written language is transactional in function and designed to be received by nonfamiliars, so too is that kind of talk known as referential communication. It is the kind of talk needed for communication when we are not at home among those who know us and recognize what we are likely to mean and how we typically express ourselves. As such, it is the obvious kind of talk required of most of those who are using an

L2 to accomplish some transactional goal, whether in education, business, technical communication, or in any of the extremely wide range of contexts where a language, such as English (as an L2), has become a common lingua franca.

Although the boundaries between interpersonal communication and referential communication can easily become blurred, it is useful for research purposes not to underestimate their distinct properties. It is certainly not the case, for example, that we only see the standard turn-taking structure of conversation in interpersonal communication. It is also present in referential communication. However, whereas participants in interpersonal talk may equally take turns, interrupt, nominate topics, and chat casually with no apparent goal, those participating in referential communication will typically be more focused, in their turns and topics, on reaching a preestablished goal of information transfer or exchange. One by-product of this goal-directed talk is that individuals can often take quite extended turns, particularly when the task (by design or not) has resulted in a predominantly one-way flow of information.

In interpersonal talk among familiars, it is unlikely that many genuine requests for clarification by the participants will be found. In such talk, the details of the message are rarely an issue, but acting as if the speaker is difficult to understand would be a serious issue. In social terms, a request for clarification is a repair mechanism (i.e., something needs to be fixed) initiated by the other (not the self), and represents one of the least-preferred ways of responding to talk. In interpersonal terms, asking *What?* or *What did you say?* may risk being face-threatening, whereas in terms of referential communication, it may simply reflect an aspect of the joint purpose of accomplishing clear message transfer.

It is also worth remembering that both types of communication are socially based. It may be that, in interpersonal communication, much more is at stake in terms of personal relationships and social connection, but there is a broader concept of social responsibility also involved when information has to be communicated. It is a social challenge, in referential communication, for the participants to take careful account of each other's perspectives. Whereas the information to be transferred or exchanged may be objectively identifiable, the way in which it is communicated is inevitably determined by the subjective involvement of the participants. More technically, it can only be communicated if some level of intersubjectivity is established (cf. Schegloff, 1992; Schiffrin, 1990). That is, each participant has to create, to a greater or lesser extent, a relevant image of the other's knowledge-state and beliefs, and constantly monitor what is said and done to maintain that image. It is, however, typically a short-term image, relevant only for the task at hand. The skillful use of referential communication is consequently tied to the individual's capacity to recognize exactly what is required by the task at hand.

Before moving on to investigate exactly what might be specified as "the task at hand" on any occasion, it is worth considering briefly what was learned from those early L1 explorations in the development of referential communication.

FURTHER READING

General reviews of work undertaken in the referential communication research tradition can be found in Asher (1979), Dickson (1982), Glucksberg, Krauss, and Higgins (1975), Lloyd (1990), Lloyd, Boada, and Forns (1992), and the contributions in Dickson (1981). On the general characteristics and relevance of tasks in L2 studies, see Crookes (1986), Foley (1991), Kumaravadivelu (1991), Long (1985, 1989, 1997), Long and Crookes (1992, 1993), Nunan (1989), Prabhu (1987), Sheen (1994), Skehan (1996), and the contributions in collections edited by Candlin and Murphy (1987), Crookes and Gass (1993a, 1993b), and Day (1986). The relevant aspects of Piaget's work can be explored in Boden (1979), Bryant (1982), Cox (1980), Ginsburg and Opper (1988), Gruber and Voneche (1977), Levin (1986), Piaget (1951), and Sutherland (1992). Aspects of Vygotsky's views related to contemporary thinking about the nature of language acquisition can be found in Cazden (1992), Vygotsky (1962, 1978), Wertsch (1985), the contributions in Moll (1990),

Rogoff and Wertsch (1984), and Wertsch (1985), and, with a specific focus on L2 research, in Frawley and Lantolf (1985), Lantolf and Ahmed (1989), and Lantolf and Appel (1994).

Research studies related to the social versus nonsocial speech distinction are reported in Garmiza and Anisfeld (1976), Garvey and Hogan (1973), Glucksberg and Krauss (1967), Glucksberg, Krauss, and Weisberg (1966), Krauss and Bricker (1967), Krauss and Glucksberg (1969), Krauss and Rotter (1968), Krauss, Vivekananthan, and Weinheimer (1968), Krauss and Weinheimer (1964, 1966, 1967), Rubin (1976), and Sachs and Devin (1976).

The importance of communicative competence as a crucial concept in much of this discussion cannot be underestimated. The origins can be found in Hymes (1971, 1972, 1974), and the application to L2 studies can be traced through Canale and Swain (1980), Celce-Murcia, Dörnyei, and Thurrell (1995), Taylor (1988), and the contributions in Richards and Schmidt (1985) and Scarcella, Andersen, and Krashen (1990). Attempts to produce operational definitions of the concept, principally for L2 testing purposes, can be found in Bachman and Palmer (1985), Canale (1988), Duran, Canale, Penfield, Stansfield, and Liskin-Gasparro (1985), and Swain (1984). Accounts of L1 acquisition can be studied in Bates, Bretherton, and Snyder (1988), Bloom (1991, 1993), Clark (1993), Goodluck (1991), Ingram (1989), and contributions in collections edited by Fletcher and Garman (1986), Franklin and Barten (1988), Messer and Turner (1993), Slobin (1985), and Wanner and Gleitman (1983). Overviews of L2 acquisition can be found in Ellis (1985, 1987b, 1994), Gass and Selinker (1994), Larsen-Freeman and Long (1991), Lightbown and Spada (1993), and Sharwood-Smith (1994). For more on Monitor Theory, read Krashen (1981, 1982, 1985) and on what might be wrong with it, see the summary of criticisms in Larsen-Freeman and Long (1991). For more information on the Teachability Hypothesis, read Pienemann (1985, 1987, 1989), Pienemann and Johnston (1987), and on its shortcomings, see Hudson (1993). On the distinction between structural and functional perspectives on language, consider Bates and

MacWhinney (1982), Croft (1995), Givón (1979, 1995), Lock (1996), Newmeyer (1991), Nichols (1984), and Thompson (1991); with specific reference to L2 studies, see Bates and MacWhinney (1981), Cooreman and Kilborn (1991), Givón (1984), Huebner (1983), Pfaff (1987a), and Tomlin (1990). The emphasis on failure to acquire nativelike L2 ability is prevalent in Hyltenstam (1992), Johnson and Newport (1989), Long (1990, 1993), Schachter (1990), and Scovel (1988). Standard L2 research methods and expectations are described in a number of general texts such as Brown (1988), Hatch and Lazaraton (1991), Johnson (1992), and Seliger and Shohamy (1989). Different perspectives on relevant L2 research methods are presented in Cumming (1994), Eisenstein, Wolfson, Henning, and Chaudron (1986), and Tarone, Gass, and Cohen (1994).

Discussions of the importance of sociocultural considerations in L2 learning can be followed up in Fiksdal (1989, 1990), Preston (1989), Sato (1990), Scollon and Scollon (1995), Tarone (1987, 1988), Wolfson (1989), and the contributions in Gass, Madden, Preston, and Selinker (1989a, 1989b), and Wolfson and Judd (1983). The impact of differences in cross-cultural values is recognized in Clyne (1994), Ochs (1982, 1988), Wierzbicka (1991), and the contributions in Kasper (1995) and Olesky (1989). On awareness of pragmatic knowledge, see Schmidt (1993).

On the nature of reference, read the overviews presented in chapter 7 of Lyons (1977) and chapter 3 of Yule (1996). For more detailed treatments of specific issues relevant to how reference works, try Bruner (1983), Fauconnier (1994), Givón (1989), Nunberg (1977), or Roberts (1993). On research into collaboration in reference, see Clark and Wilkes-Gibbs (1986), Clark and Schaefer (1987a, 1989), Garrod and Anderson (1987), Goodwin (1981), Schober and Clark (1989), Wilkes-Gibbs (1995, 1997), and Wilkes-Gibbs and Clark (1992).

On approximating and vague language, see Channell (1994), Dines (1980), Stubbs (1986a), Wachtel (1980), and Wierzbicka (1986). On the related concept of core vocabulary, see Carter (1987) or Stubbs (1986b). On the extremely important topic of categorization processes, see chapter 2 of Barsalou (1992) for an overview, or Rosch (1977, 1983), Rosch and Mervis (1975), and the contributions in Neisser (1987) or Rosch and Lloyd (1978). On ad hoc categorization, see Barsalou (1983) and Overstreet and Yule (1997).

There are many texts providing basic treatments of communication, such as Dimbleby and Burton (1992), Ellis and McClintock (1994), and King (1989). Sperber and Wilson (1986) distinguish between a code model and an inferential model of communication. A good review of communication issues relevant to child development and referential communication is presented in Shatz (1983). On the use of a lingua franca in communication, see Wagner and Firth (1997).

Interpersonal communication is really the province of interactional sociolinguistics, which has developed into a huge field. The major sources are Goffman (1967, 1974, 1981) and Gumperz (1982a, 1982b), whose earlier work is collected in Dil (1971). Applications of their ideas can be found in work by Brown and Levinson (1987), Schiffrin (1987), and Tannen (1984, 1989). Schiffrin (1994) provides overviews of several related areas. More specifically, on the background to concepts such as reciprocity of perspectives, see Cicourel (1974), Garfinkel (1967), Heritage (1984), Husserl (1978), Schütz (1962), and Schütz and Luckmann (1977); on intersubjectivity, read Schegloff (1992) and Schiffrin (1990). Aston (1993), Rampton (1997), and van Lier (1996) situate some of these issues in L2 contexts. On the analysis of the structure of interaction, there are a number of recent texts, for example, Psathas (1995), Stenström (1994), Taylor and Cameron (1987), and Tsui (1994). Most of the original insights are to be found in Sacks (1992).

2

The Development of (L1) Referential Communication

The vast majority of L1 studies in referential communication involve children between 4 and 8 years of age. The most consistent observation, echoing Piaget (1959), is that the referential communication abilities of 7- to 8-year-olds are qualitatively and quantitatively different from those of 4- to 5-year-olds. Something happens to children that starts to become manifest in the use of language some time around their sixth year. We look first at some of the details of this observed change and then review some of the explanations.

SOME BASIC FINDINGS

Both production (speaking) and judgment (listening) tasks are used. The typical production task requires the child to describe verbally one item from an array of similar items so that a listener (real or imaginary) can identify it. The array may contain toy figures holding or wearing different things, or pictures of shapes such as triangles or circles that differ in color, size, and design. There are also judgment tasks in which the children hear a description and (usually) have to point to the item being described or indicate that they cannot select an item on the basis of the description. In these types of studies, an effective message, containing explicit information that allows one item to be uniquely identified, is treated as *nonambiguous*, and an ineffective message, containing insufficient information for unique identification, is described as *ambiguous*.

The general finding is that younger children (4 to 5 years) commonly produce, and react to, ambiguous messages as if they were unambiguous. This finding is extremely robust, having been noted in a large number of studies (cf. Alvy, 1968; Cosgrove & Patterson, 1977; Ironsmith & Whitehurst, 1978a; Patterson & Kister, 1981; Robinson, 1981; Sodian, 1988; Whitehurst & Sonnenschein, 1978). This phenomenon does not seem to be the result of random guessing or linguistic ignorance. It is remarkably consistent according to the following type of pattern: If the message contains the word *flower*, it is judged by younger children to be effective for identifying a red flower, even when a blue flower is also in the array, but a message containing the word *flag* is judged to be ineffective (Robinson & Robinson, 1977). The normal interpretation of such observations is that younger children only require messages to be consistent with referents (Whitehurst & Sonnenschein, 1981) and that the potential ambiguity of some messages is simply not even heard. Indeed, they will later accept an unambiguous message as being identical to an ambiguous version already accepted as adequate (Robinson & Robinson, 1982).

There are, however, some observations that suggest that the ambiguous and unambiguous messages are not actually being treated as the same. For example, ambiguous messages often create longer reaction times (Bearison & Levey, 1977), are accompanied by more hand and eye movements (Patterson, Cosgrove, & O'Brien, 1980), and are treated very differently when the children are told that the speaker is not to be trusted (Ackerman, 1981a). Even when they indicate that an ambiguous message is good enough for identifying one item, the children can actually go on to talk about the number of different referents that the ambiguous message identifies (Robinson & Robinson, 1983). Feedback also has a definite impact (Peterson, Danner, & Flavell, 1972; Sonnenschein, 1984). Thus, even while displaying apparent ignorance of criterial properties of effective referential communication, younger children seem to have some latent sense of the existence of a variable relationship between meaning intended and meaning conveyed. Because that dormant ability appears to be fully available and in use by the time those children are 7 to 8 years old, some explanation of what triggers the change has been sought.

SOME EXPLANATIONS

The simplest explanation for their better communicative performance is that older children have passed through some kind of maturational stage. This type of nativist explanation (i.e., it is biologically predetermined) also assumes uniformity of effect, in the sense that all "normal" children will progress in the same age-related way, regardless of situation, experience, training, or any other variable effect. We might just call it "a natural development." Although this account may be the simplest, it doesn't actually explain very much. Two types of observations may help us understand the nature of what triggers this change in communicative performance. Researchers have noted that training does have an effect and that the situation where some training typically occurs for most children also has a profound impact on language use.

A number of specific training (or *intervention*) studies have been described. Explicitly asking younger children to evaluate the performances of two dolls as effective communicators had the effect of changing the children's ability to produce and identify unambiguous messages (Sonnenschein & Whitehurst, 1984). Verbal feedback such as repeatedly asking the children to reformulate their utterances until they were clearly unambiguous also resulted in improvement (Lefebvre-Pinard, Charbonneau, & Feider, 1982). Also, verbal feedback that explicitly indicated the kind of problem the listener was facing with ambiguous messages (e.g., *but there are four like that*) resulted in improved judgments and performance (Robinson & Robinson, 1981). As Robinson and Whittaker (1986) pointed out, in studies of this type, "children are encouraged to behave 'as if' they already understand about both ambiguity and its role in causing communication failure" (p. 163). Without that encouragement, the children may simply operate with no awareness of communication failure.

The next question is: Where do children get that encouragement? Interestingly, they do not typically get it at home. When transcripts of children's natural language experiences at home are studied for any evidence of younger children being asked to reformulate ambiguous utterances or to show that they are aware of the problems of ambiguous utterances, there is little to be found. At home, younger children's referential communication is mostly treated as transparent. That is, what they say is generally interpreted as fulfilling what they mean to say, whether or not it actually would do so for an external observer (Wells, 1986a). However, the transcripts of children's language experiences at school reveal many instances where children are challenged to make their utterances more explicit and are required to demonstrate that they have clearly understood exactly what was said to them. It may just be that school, like other institutional worlds, attaches much more importance to effective referential communication.

The early school experiences of children contain many incidental training events where an intuitively simple response to a question is discouraged in favor of a more complex, explicit response. Notice, in the following example (from MacLure & French, 1981, p. 212), how the teacher directs the child (Rosie, aged 5) to *tell* her what can be seen in the pictures rather than accepting Rosie's response that the teacher can look for herself.

Teacher: What can you see?
Rosie: And they're going in the sand.
Teacher: Mm.
Rosie: You have a look.
Teacher: Well you have a look and tell me.
           I've seen it already.
           I want to see if you can see.

In this example, the teacher makes it clear that the task is not to inform the teacher (who already knows what's in the pictures), but to be verbally explicit about what is already known.

Teachers also force children to pay attention to extended sequences of instructions and often ask children explicitly to repeat parts of the message if the children seem to have misunderstood the intended meaning. Teachers frequently ask display questions (i.e., already knowing the answer), giving them the opportunity to evaluate whether the children actually understood what has been said, as it was intended. Teachers are also professionally involved in getting children to pay attention to language itself, not only in spoken language tasks, but crucially in those activities designed to foster literacy (cf. Donaldson, 1978). For some commentators (e.g., Wells, 1986b), the most salient difference for children entering the classroom world is the virtual disappearance of interest in what they personally might try to talk about. The expression of a personal perspective is typically neither acknowledged nor encouraged. The teacher's chosen topic and perspective dominate. In many ways, coping with early schooling would seem to depend on an ability to see things from the teacher's perspective.

Before their sixth year, the majority of children go through a major social transition from a familiar environment (home) where most messages are readily understood because their intended meanings are largely predictable (and communication failure has few consequences) to an institutional environment (school) where most messages have to be attended to more carefully in order to be understood (and communication failure has larger consequences). It would seem that the "natural" development coincides with a major sociocultural change in the child's status and experience of language use, particularly with regard to referential communication.

As a number of researchers have pointed out (Flavell, Speer, Green, & August, 1981; Lloyd & Beveridge, 1981; Markman, 1981), there is an additional cognitive processing requirement created in this new environment. Much more information processing and representation, particularly of a decontextualized type, is expected (cf. Temple, Wu, & Snow, 1991). There is a need to cope with information that is not part of the shared context (i.e., the immediate here and now). Indeed, the most basic aspect of this development may be a change in cognitive representation demanded of an organism that is spending more time using independent movement to encounter nonfamiliar environments. The child is spending much more time away from family and home. Developing better referential communication skills may simply be a by-product of becoming responsible for analyzing all environmental phenomena more carefully.

Rather than view the development of more effective referential communication skills in children as having a single source, we might see it as multidimensional (maturational, social, and cognitive). Having looked at how we get from poorer referential communication skills at 4 to 5 years to better skills at 7 to 8 years, the next question is whether the development of referential communication skills is complete at that point? Apparently, it is not.

LATER DEVELOPMENTS

In a much-quoted paper, Krauss and Glucksberg (1969) reported that the age-related development of communicative ability does not, in their terms, "reveal any abrupt discontinuity in proficiency" (p. 263). They reported a gradual development through the age range from 5- to 10-year-olds, confirming a similar earlier finding (Glucksberg & Krauss, 1967). Pechman and Deutsch (1982) found the same pattern for referential descriptions. Lloyd (1990) also reported that 10-year-olds were significantly better than 7-year-olds in terms of communicative success on a task. Krauss and Glucksberg (1969) had earlier noted that the performance of 14-year-olds was still inferior to that of adults. Clearly, the development of referential communication ability is not tied to only one critical period in childhood.

It is worth noting that the reported findings just mentioned are based on the average score for a group at a particular age level. Sometimes when groups of children, say 7-year-olds and 13-year-olds, are compared, there can be interesting observations beyond simply recounting differences in average scores. The spread of the scores is typically not reported, but it turns out to be very revealing. In assessing overall communicative performance on a task, Anderson, Clark, and Mullin (1994) found variation within their age groups: "For example, 25% of performances from seven-year-olds are more successful than the average performance of thirteen-year-olds and 25% of the performances of thirteen-year-olds are worse than the average performance of seven-year-olds" (p. 457).

This represents one of the few technical reports that document a rather simple fact: the development of effective communication skills in the L1 is not automatic. Wright and Hull (1990) came to a similar conclusion. In this aspect of language development, older does not necessarily mean better. Earlier studies of very low levels of task-related communicative ability among teenagers (14- and 15-year-olds) were reported in Brown, Anderson, Shillcock, and Yule (1984). Brown, Sharkey, and Brown (1987) reported a similar finding and attributed it, in their study, to some limitations in information-processing capacity (i.e., poor working memory) among "less able" teenagers. Although it is occasionally noted that certain aspects of L1 linguistic knowledge are relatively late acquisitions for most children (cf. Karmiloff-Smith, 1986; Romaine, 1984), the possibility that large numbers of older children, and even adults, have not developed effective referential communication skills in speaking their L1 is rarely mentioned and hardly ever researched.

Whether such observations are relevant or not for L1 studies, they do represent a serious omission from the perspective of L2 studies. Specifically, no preexisting assumption of L1 communicative effectiveness should be automatically made for either the L2 learner (in his or her L1) or the native speaker of the target language. Certainly, the frequent assumption of perfect L1 linguistic competence of native speakers found in linguistic studies of L2 acquisition cannot be extended to studies of referential communication. Any referential communication studies are essentially required to collect comparable data of performance on task by native speakers of the target (matched along some reasonable dimension).

Even with this precaution, however, there is no guarantee that the very concept of effective communication can be treated as a stable construct across groups taking part in research projects. Nor should we assume, in principle, that an ability to perform a communicative task effectively in the L1 will necessarily be available in the L2. There is, after all, the "foreign language effect" (Takano & Noda, 1995; p. 658) that results in a temporary decline in processing ability when "demanding cognitive tasks are performed in parallel" (Norman & Bobrow, 1975; p. 46). Ricard and Snow (1990) reported a similar observation. We do know that apparent L1 ability in performing a communicative task, at a specific age, can disappear if a more cognitively demanding version of the task is presented. Generalizing, after more than a decade of referential communication research with children, Krauss and Glucksberg (1977) included an analogy with the use of foreigner talk in their summation of how social and nonsocial speech are subject to the communicative stress of a situation:

When the demands of the task become heavy enough, children may not have the opportunity to bring into play the social communication skills they possess. If this seems strange, it is well to keep in mind that even mature and articulate adults can find themselves in situations where they fail to take another person's knowledge and perspective into account. Consider the American tourist in a foreign country who asks, "Where is the men's room?" and, on receiving no answer because his informant speaks no English, proceeds to shout, "Men's room, toilet, where?" Such an adult is not very different from the child who tries to communicate an unfamiliar geometric form by calling it "Daddy's shirt." Both the tourist and the child are ordinarily able to distinguish social from nonsocial speech and to communicate socially, and yet both may find themselves so overwhelmed by the demands of the particular situation that they do not bring that ability into play." (pp. 104–105)

Whether or not we agree that these two situations are as similar as the authors believe, there is little doubt that the general observation about communicative demands is a valid one. In the course of the following chapters, we explore some sources of this observed variability in performance as they emerge in the use of referential communication tasks in L2 research.

FURTHER READING

Further details of earlier L1 research on referential communication can be found in Ackerman (1981b), Asher and Oden (1976), Asher and Parke (1975), Beal and Flavell (1982), Bearison and Cassell (1975), Bredart (1984), Camaioni and Ercolani (1988), Ford and Olson (1975), Jackson and Jacobs (1982), Maratsos (1973), McTear (1987), Pascual-Leone and Smith (1969), Patterson, Massad, and Cosgrove (1978), Patterson and Roberts (1982), Ratner and Rice (1963), Roberts and Patterson (1983), Robinson and Robinson (1976), Robinson and Whittaker (1987), Shatz and Gelman (1973), Simons and Murphy (1986), Singer and Flavell (1981), and Surian and Job (1987). Some more recent studies are reported in Anderson, Clark, and Mullin (1991), Higgins (1992), Lloyd (1991, 1992), Mitchell and Russell (1991), Reeder, Shapiro, Watson, and Goelman (1996), and Robinson (1994). For more information on training, or intervention, studies, see Asher and Wigfield (1981), Brown et al. (1984), Fry (1966), Ironsmith and Whitehurst (1978b), Markman and Gorin (1981), Patterson and Kister (1981), Shantz (1981), Shantz and Wilson (1972), and Whitehurst (1976). On the broader aspects of cognitive development, see Flavell, Miller, and Miller (1993) and Flavell and Ross (1981). The relationship between referential communication skills and language or learning impairment is explored in Bishop and Adams (1991), Donahue, Pearl, and Bryan (1982), Hubbell (1981), Meline (1986), Noel (1980), and Spekman (1981). On studies of language at home and in school, see MacLure and French (1981), McTear (1985), Wells (1985a, 1985b, 1985c, 1986a, 1986b), Wood (1988), and Wood, McMahon, and Cranstoun (1980). Studies of linguistic development in older children are reported in Chomsky (1969), Clark (1971, 1993), Durkin (1981, 1986), Emerson and Getkowski (1980), and Litowitz and Novy (1984).

3

Principles and Distinctions

There is a great deal about the nature of L2 referential communication research and its typical tasks that is best explained in terms of a reaction against previous formats and materials. Investigating language acquisition via mechanical devices and fixed response formats appeared to belong to a very restricted perspective on both the nature of language and the process of acquisition. Multiple-choice response formats, fill-in-the-blank exercises, "repeat-after-me" imitation modes, grammaticality judgments, and other related measures all seemed to be too restrictive. Valuable though such instruments have proved to be in the investigation of L2 morpho-syntax, they typically require participants to react to decontextualized stimuli rather than produce their own expressions in a communicative context. In contrast, it is an interest in considering what L2 speakers have to say and how they actually say it that has prompted much of the task-based research. This interest has also led to the development of speaking–listening (rather than reading–writing) materials and a preference for discourse (rather than sentential) data.

Emerging in a number of different ways during the early 1980s, L2 research involving communicative tasks began to establish a number of design principles. In many ways, these principles evolved from a desire to design tasks in such a way that a certain type of data would be recorded. Although there was a broad goal to elicit and record spoken discourse, there was also an early realization that a distinction would have to be drawn between casual interpersonal communication (as in everyday informal conversation) and referential communication (as in transactional tasks). From a research perspective, there were too many uncontrolled variables involved in casual chat and it did not become a site for much referential communication research. As researchers began to specify more precisely what kind of control they wanted, some simple principles became clear and generally accepted. Some others continue to be the subject of discussion and may best be characterized as design *distinctions* rather than principles. We first review some of those basic principles and then explore the kind of design issues that are still the subject of discussion.

PRINCIPLES

Referential communication research is about communication, hence someone has to be attempting intentionally to transfer some information to someone else in the course of the task. It follows that the researcher should always be trying to accomplish the following:

1. *Elicit speech that has a purpose.* This principle is, in essence, a requirement that someone is listening (or will listen) to what the speaker is attempting to communicate. That listener must also have a task to perform on the basis of the speaker's talk. The speaker has to be given some sense that what is being said, and how it is said, will have an impact on how successfully the task of the listener can be accomplished.

2. *Elicit extended discourse.* Unlike many traditional classroom exercises, the referential communication task should put the speaker in control of the floor, in charge of the information flow, and responsible for the effectiveness of the communication. The task should require extended talk and not brief responses.

3. *Elicit structured discourse.* The extended talk should be structured effectively so that the listener's task can be accomplished successfully. Task design can and should provide some basic structural organization and a completion point.

4. *Elicit controlled discourse.* The researcher determines what the participants will talk about, either via topic or task type. The

general topics (*What did you do during spring break?*) of class-room talk are not effective task-based prompts, largely because the goal of such talk is undefined and open to widely different interpretations. By providing the task materials, the researcher controls to a large extent the type of discourse (e.g., descriptive or narrative) that will be recorded. This procedure also deter-mines, for example, how many characters there are in a story, what they are like, and what happens to them.

5. *Elicit the speaker's discourse.* Although the content of tasks is broadly controlled, there is no predetermined set of linguistic forms designated for use in referential communication tasks. In this respect, the tasks differ quite significantly from many other research instruments. It is certainly possible to design tasks that create a likely use (or abuse) of certain linguistic forms, but the basic formats typically do not prescribe linguistic choices.

6. *Elicit a range of discourses.* As much as possible, the re-searcher should try to use different task types to elicit (and record) descriptions, instructions, directions, and narrative ac-counts, in order to arrive at a profile of the range of a speaker's ability.

These principles are intended to provide a speaker with some pre-selected information to convey, a listener who requires that information in order to complete a task, and an awareness that an information gap exists. In following these principles, re-searchers hope to motivate the participants, achieving some degree of involvement, attention, and interest, while eliciting a wide range of extended L2 discourse on content already known to the researcher and thereby allowing the analysis of how that content was expressed. There is one other principle that relates more to what the researcher (rather than the participant) has to do. It is concerned with data:

7. *Elicit baseline data.* For L2 studies, the baseline data is task performance in the L1. There are two possible dimensions to this requirement. In most previous studies, the baseline data requirement has been met via recordings of native speakers of the target performing the same tasks as the L2 speakers. This dimension is designed to ensure that nonnative speaker per-

formance will be viewed relative to actual native speaker performance rather than some assumed or idealized target performance. Such baseline data elicitation also allows the researcher to determine how native speakers (of the target) react to the demands of the task. The other dimension of the baseline data requirement is tied to an increasing interest in how L2 speakers would perform the task in their own L1. That is, for the participants, the relevant baseline data may be their own native language performance on that type of task.

Ideally, both types of baseline data would be gathered, but this may not always be practical. Even a small pilot use of the task, however, is extremely valuable. In many task-related research projects, more specific types of data are often sought, and hence create particular requirements on the nature of task design. This leads to a number of important distinctions.

DISTINCTIONS

Discussions of distinctions in using referential communication tasks for research purposes can be divided into two broad areas: task formats and participant roles. Other issues, more specifically concerned with materials and procedures, are considered in the following chapter.

Task Formats

One way of distinguishing between tasks is in terms of information flow. The task can be designed to create a one-way flow of information from one speaker to the other, essentially a process of information transfer, or a *two-way* flow from each to the other, in a process of information exchange. The two-way format gives both speakers "potentially equal control over the information" (Pica, Lincoln-Porter, Paninos, & Linnell, 1996, p. 68). It is also sometimes called a jigsaw design, and can be further divided in terms of information suppliance. The design can determine whether information exchange is either optional or required within task performance.

An additional distinction is sometimes noted between the communicative goals assigned to participants by the task format. There may be a convergent effect, essentially requiring participants to reach a common goal or solution that they agree on, or there may be a divergent effect, in which the task creates different, even conflicting, goals for the participants. This is also sometimes described as a distinction between tasks fostering collaboration versus independence in goal orientation. A combination of some of these factors is sometimes used to characterize tasks as *open* (no required information exchange, no defined solution) or *closed* (information exchange and common solution required).

Although these distinctions are generally discussed as if they were aspects of the tasks themselves, they are actually task requirements. As several commentators (e.g., Brown, 1989; Duff, 1993; Hulstijn, 1989) have noted, it is not always the case that the researcher's ideas of task requirements are matched by those of the participants (as evidenced by their performance on the task). Task outcomes inevitably depend on the participants being able to recognize what the researcher expects them to do. Consequently, some attention must always be paid to those participants and their roles.

Participant Roles

Whereas early referential communication research involved children (and L1 development), the L2 research has mostly been conducted with older participants, typically of college age. It has also included diverse pairings of native (NS) and nonnative (NNS) speakers of a language. Although it has not been the subject of much discussion, the distinction between L2 context (within an L2 community) and a foreign language context (within an L1 community) is worth keeping in mind, particularly with regard to cultural assumptions about the whole business of taking part in tasks for research purposes. In English-as-a-second-language contexts, for example, student participants may have become much more familiar with tasks than in English-as-a-foreign-language contexts.

The most basic technical aspect of participant role is the assignment of who will do what in the task. Conventionally, one participant is simply the speaker and the other is the listener (but listeners can usually speak too). As Krauss and Fussell (1990) put it, speakers are "the individuals who initiate messages" (p. 114). When the roles are more defined, these can become sender (of information) and receiver.

Alternative labels, found in instructional or direction-giving tasks, are director and matcher (Schober, 1995), explainer and follower (Blakar, 1984), instructor and instructee (Lloyd, 1991), or information giver and information follower (Anderson, Clark, and Mullen, 1994). Depending on other aspects of the task design, these labels often simply reflect a nominal assignment at the beginning of a task and do not necessarily establish power or dominance. However, it should be recognized that there is a certain kind of power assigned to whoever holds more task-related information than the other (as in many instructional tasks).

There is power associated with status, such as being designated the expert in a task, talking to a novice. There is also power that will typically come from being the higher proficiency L2 speaker, working with a lower proficiency speaker, and, by extension, being an NS versus an NNS. For many participants, there also appears to be a gender effect, in that the task performance of males together may differ from females together, and also that same gender pairs (male–male, female–female) should not be assumed to be the same as mixed gender pairs (male–female). Also, familiarity of the participants with each other and with the type of task must be kept in mind. In some research, the differences between referential communication addressed to friends versus strangers has been explored (cf. Krauss, 1987). One form of familiarity can simply be familiarity with one role in the task, as when a participant who has been a receiver of information in one version of a task is then put in the role of sender. This role-related effect (receiver-then-sender) may be greater than if the participant is a sender in one version of the task and then repeats the sender role in another version.

Many of these role-related aspects have not been given sufficient attention in previous research, often being ignored or simply noted as isolated variables. It is important to keep in mind that, at any point in task performance, each participant's contribution may be a reflection of any one, or even a complex combination, of a range of interacting role-related variables.

FURTHER READING

On the value of task as opposed to other instruments used in acquisition research, see Long (1985, 1997), Long and Crookes (1993), and Nunan (1993). On the origins of discourse-focused research, see Hatch (1978b) or the review of developments in Pica (1994). For more background on the principles listed here, see Brown et al. (1984), Brown and Yule (1983), Long and Sato (1984), and Tarone and Yule (1989). On the idea of an information gap task, see Davies (1982) and Doughty and Pica (1986) and, for an overview of several task format distinctions, see Pica, Kanagy, and Falodun (1993). More specifically, on the use of one- and two-way tasks, see Long (1981, 1983c), on the concept of a jigsaw task, see Geddes (1981) and Johnson (1981), on the convergent–divergent distinction, see Duff (1986), and on open versus closed versions, see Long (1989). For distinctions between task and task requirements, see Duff (1993) and Hulstijn (1989). On cultural assumptions and task performance, see Hall (1993) and Jorden (1992). Task-based research on status (expert vs. novice) can be found in Alkire, Collum, Kaswan, and Love (1968), Isaacs and Clark (1987), Woken and Swales (1989), and Zuengler (1989a, 1989b, 1993). Proficiency effects are discussed in Varonis and Gass (1985b), Yule (1990a), and Yule and Macdonald (1990). Gender effects are noted in Gass and Varonis (1986), Markham (1988), and Pica, Holliday, Lewis, and Morgenthaler (1989). The issue of familiarity is explored in Gass and Varonis (1984) and Plough and Gass (1993). Another role-related distinction, that between addressee and overhearer, results in differences in communication, according to Clark and Schaefer (1987b) and Schober and Clark (1989). The effect of role change, or the listener effect, is reported in Anderson, Yule, and Brown (1984) for L1, and Yule (1991) for L2. Other listener effects have been explored in Brown and Dell (1987), Fussell and Krauss (1989), Graumann and Hermann (1988), Krauss and Fussell (1988), Kraut, Lewis, and Swezey (1982), and Schober (1995).

4

Materials and Procedures

The materials used in referential communication tasks are typically visual and nonverbal. That is, diagrams, drawings, photographs, and pictures are generally selected or designed for use in the tasks, whereas textual material, or any type of written language, is mostly avoided. Physical objects or parts of objects (to be identified or assembled) are also used, as well as toys and components of construction games. Although it is rarely discussed, the primary assumption underlying these choices seems to be tied to a preference for eliciting the participants' own language, in a fairly spontaneous way, rather than prompting or priming them to use provided language. It also seems to be considered an advantage that such materials are *proficiency neutral*, to the extent that no participant is required to cope with potentially unfamiliar or puzzling written language in the materials. In this way, problems related to literacy levels are also minimized. With regard to spoken language proficiency, these materials allow participants to use whatever L2 knowledge they possess (or can recall) during task performance.

The same (nonverbal) materials are also *language neutral* in the sense that they can be used with any L1 and L2 pairs. To a large extent, they are also *age neutral*, allowing the same task to be conducted with young children, teenagers, and adults. Some materials can, however, seem more for children than others (e.g., Lego toys). Some will even appear to be more gender biased (e.g., kitchen utensils or tools) for those who assume traditional gender roles. A large range of potential issues related to covert social and cultural bias may actually be involved in the selection of a particular type of material for referential communication tasks. Such issues have not received the serious attention they deserve in most previous research and are certain to be the focus of more careful consideration in the future. In research, it is worth remembering that "all findings are captives of the methods by which they are obtained" (Shantz, 1975, p. 15).

MATERIALS AS DESIGNED

Before discussing different examples of materials, we should note that we are, at this point, discussing the materials as designed and not as actually performed on a specific occasion. Overwhelmingly, the way in which the materials are designed to be used (following trials and pilot exercises) is reflected directly in how they are actually used by participants in performing the tasks. However, there are inevitable occasions when participants do not appear to be following the material designer's expectations. On one occasion, a speaker appeared to be treating the individual frames in a cartoon strip sequence (cf. Fig. 4.18A) almost as if they were unrelated. Instead of producing the expected story, the speaker provided several separate scene descriptions (or so it seemed). Brown (1989) and Duff (1993) reported on similar experiences. In such a case (and potentially in the use of any task materials), the participant's interpretation of the task requirements may not match the task designer's expectations.

IDENTIFICATION, NAMING, AND DESCRIBING

The most basic materials used for referential communication contain a single entity to be identified, or distinguished from a group of other entities. That entity may be a physical object, or a drawing or photograph. For some research projects, real world objects are used, but for others, abstract figures are preferred.

Real-World Objects

Perhaps the most basic materials for an identification task are pictures of real-world objects that the speaker can see and the listener cannot. The speaker has to name or describe each pictured object in such a way that the listener is able to identify it. For example, working with "colored photographs of familiar objects such as *a bib, an abacus* and *a car*" (Poulisse & Schils, 1989, p. 19), one group of investigators produced a number of research reports on the referential communication of Dutch L1 speakers using English as their L2 (cf. Poulisse, 1987, 1990; Poulisse and Bongaerts, 1994; Poulisse, Bongaerts, & Kellerman, 1987). As another example, in a study of L1 referential communication (involving U. S. university students), Isaacs and Clark (1987) used picture postcards of a number of different scenes in New York. Clearly, a very wide range of possible pictures could be employed as materials in this basic type of identification task.

If, however, the context is more limited and the goal of the exercise is, for example, to elicit some simple classroom vocabulary, then an array of typical classroom objects (e.g., pen, pencil, ruler, sharpener) can be presented, physically or in a photograph, in order to elicit simple L2 labels for one or more of the objects. This kind of naming exercise is often embedded in a task that requires the speaker to describe a set of objects lying on a table. The illustration shown in Fig. 4.1 has objects from the classroom

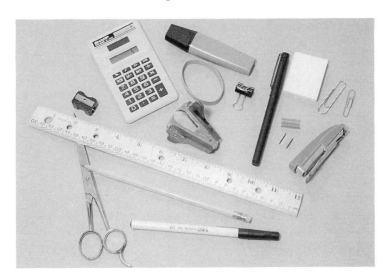

FIG. 4.1. Classroom items.

and, in Fig. 4.2, from the kitchen. Other sets of objects that have been presented in such arrays include hand tools, sports equipment, items of clothing, various toys, or even miscellaneous items, as illustrated in Loschky and Bley-Vroman (1993).

It is fairly common, in versions of this basic task, to create pairs of photographs that are almost identical except for one object. That object can be missing in one photograph or moved to a different position. The speaker's task is to describe the array of objects in such a way that the missing (or moved) entity can be identified. Research applications of this task type have been reported in Brown and Yule (1983) and Clennell (1994, 1995).

The format just described has the essential structure found in a widely used type of pedagogical exercise called "Spot the difference," one example of which is presented in Fig. 4.3A and 4.3B. Such exercises are often designed around pairs of drawings in which a variable number of small details are different. One advantage of this type of material is its general familiarity for most participants, thus reducing the need for long introductions and increasing the likelihood that all participants will approach

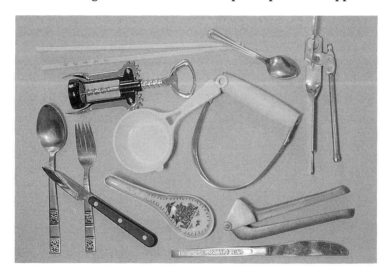

FIG. 4.2. Kitchen items.

FIG. 4.3A. Spot the difference.

FIG. 4.3B. Spot the difference.

the task in a similar way. Research applications of materials of this type are reported in Plough and Gass (1993) and Samuda and Rounds (1993).

In their performance on tasks of this type, participants may simply provide labels for some objects (*there's a telephone and a television*) and short descriptions for others (*a picture with a lightning*). The more familiar the entities to be identified, the more likely that the speakers will produce single-word labels or short phrases. In many classroom uses, the purpose of such exercises may be to provide students with the opportunity to use what they have learned, in an activity that creates relatively little stress and is designed for the students to experience success in speaking the L2 with some ease and fluency. In contrast, for many L2 research projects, the purpose of such an exercise may be to create minor problems of communication for the participants in order to investigate how they overcome the problems (or not).

One of the most basic ways to create this problematicity is to design the materials so that simple naming of objects (using familiar vocabulary) will not be sufficient for identification. If the speaker sees only a picture containing one hat and the listener has a picture containing that hat plus two or three others, then the simple expression, *it's a hat*, will not be enough. Taking Fig. 4.4 as an illustration, the speaker can be given a copy of the photograph in Fig. 4.4A and asked to describe it in order that a listener looking at the three photographs (Fig. 4.4A, B, C) will be able to identify the correct one.

As illustrated in Figs. 4.5, 4.6, and 4.7, the same basic task format can be used with objects that are less familiar in everyday experience. Reducing the familiarity of the object typically increases the difficulty of being able to identify that object with a simple word or two. There is an increase in communicative stress for the speaker. What the L2 speaker does in response to that increased communicative stress has been the focus of research, mainly in terms of communication strategies. Research applications of materials of this type are presented in Tarone and Yule (1987, 1989).

FIG. 4.4A. Hats.

FIG. 4.4B. Hats.

FIG. 4.4C. Hats.

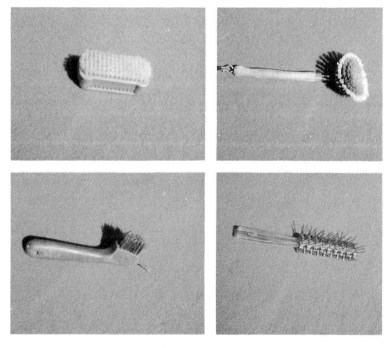

FIG. 4.5. Brushes.

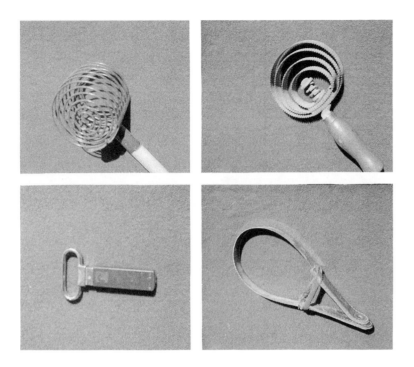

FIG. 4.6. Round things.

Abstract Figures

In designing such materials, it may not always be possible to find sets of physical objects of the types shown in Fig. 4.6 and 4.7. (These particular items were mostly found among equipment used in the care and training of horses.) An alternative approach is to use drawings, not of physical objects, but of abstract figures. One well-known set of abstract shapes is illustrated in Fig. 4.8. Different subsets from this group of what were called "graphic designs" (Krauss & Weinheimer, 1964) were used in a number of early L1 studies of referential communication. It is clear that simple labels (e.g., *hat, brush*) or short descriptions (e.g., *the round hat with stripes*) will be harder to find for such abstract shapes, mainly because the chosen designs have no conventional names.

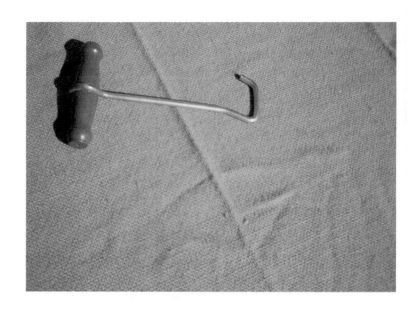

FIG. 4.7A. Hooks.

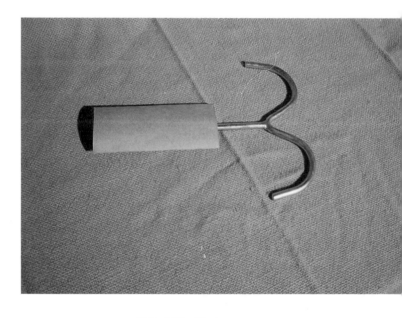

FIG. 4.7B. Hooks.

FIG. 4.7C. Hooks.

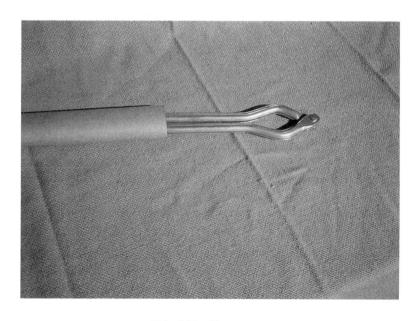

FIG. 4.7D. Hooks.

The speaker who is given one design from the set in Fig. 4.8, with the task of getting a listener to identify it from all the others, generally has to solve a quite complex communication problem. There is the cognitive dimension of analyzing the abstract shape, the social dimension of fitting that analysis to the listener's perspective, and the linguistic dimension of encoding that sociocognitive analysis. Young children in the early L1 studies (Glucksberg & Krauss, 1967) had substantial difficulty, not in naming the designs, but in naming or describing them in such a way that a partner could recognize, and hence use to identify, the one intended. For L2 speakers, the task is no less demanding, and the communication problems it appears to create have been the focus of research on L2 communication strategies. One version of the abstract figures shown in Fig. 4.8 is presented in Poulisse (1990). Other L2 research applications of this type of material have been reported in Bongaerts, Kellerman, and Bentlage (1987); Bongaerts and Poulisse (1989); Kellerman, Bongaerts, and Poulisse (1987); and Poulisse and Bongaerts (1994).

A number of other sets of graphic designs have been used to elicit descriptive language. Sometimes they resemble shapes with

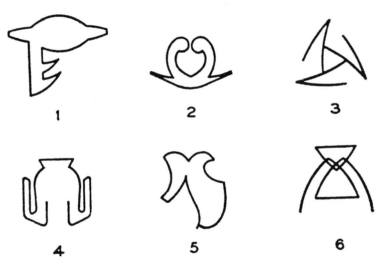

FIG. 4.8. Abstract shapes.

conventional names such as geometrical forms or letters of the alphabet, as in Kellerman, Ammerlaan, Bongaerts, and Poulisse (1990). Sometimes they have shapes that are clearly designed to defy conventional labels as much as possible, as in the so-called nonsense figures used by Krauss and Fussell (1990). Most of these designs are genuinely abstract and appear, in their creation, to have avoided any resemblance to human or animal figures.

In contrast, one set of shapes, illustrated in Fig. 4.9, does seem to consist of human-like figures. These shapes, chosen from a large collection of figures in the Chinese game of Tangram (Elffers, 1976), were cut out of black construction paper and pasted on white cards. Known simply as *tangrams*, these figures have been used in referential communication research by Clark and Wilkes-Gibbs (1986), Schober and Clark (1989), and Traxler and Gernsbacher (1995).

Words and Concepts

For all the materials described so far, the typical task use has been one in which a speaker looks at and describes one object or shape for a listener who has several objects or shapes to look at and choose from, on the basis of that description. (There are, of course, many other task uses for such materials.) There is an interesting variation on this task type that employs sets of words rather than objects or shapes. Treated as a concept identification task, this type of material demands a higher level of both literacy and proficiency than is required for most of the other (visual) materials presented so far. Basically, the speaker is given a list of words from the target language (a sample is shown as Fig. 4.10) and asked to explain each of their meanings (without using the word) so that the listener can identify the mystery word.

Concrete terms (e.g., *drum, hammock*), sometimes accompanied by pictures, and abstract terms (e.g., *flattery, sympathy*) are both presented, individually on cards and typically with L1 translation equivalents. Whereas the concrete terms (particularly with illustrations) may simply represent a variation on the visual "real-world object" task, the identification of terms for abstract concepts creates a quite different demand on the

FIG. 4.9. Tangrams.

dust pan	confidence
guitar	generosity
hammock	honesty
kite	justice
monkey	optimism
temple	persistence
thimble	pride
seesaw	success

FIG. 4.10. Words and concepts.

speaker than other identification tasks. Research reports on the use of such materials are presented in Paribakht (1985) and Chen (1990). A similar type of task requiring L1 terms (e.g., *child-care benefit* in Hungarian) to be defined in the L2 (English) has been called a "definition formulation task" (Dörnyei, 1995, p. 69). Snow (1987) also reported on the use of a related type of definition task with children in a bilingual school.

In all these identification task materials, the main interest is in how effectively or not the speaker uses available language to identify the entity. This ability is also required in instructional tasks, but there the speaker must also help the listener to create something. The materials used in instructional tasks typically require the listener to do something more than simply identify intended referents among an array of nonreferents.

INSTRUCTIONS AND DIRECTIONS

It is typically the case that an instructional task will require speakers to help listeners identify referents, as in a basic description task. However, instructional tasks may also require the listener to create referents, for example, by drawing them or assembling them. Moreover, those referents will have to be located relative to other referents being identified or created. In most materials designed for description tasks, the listener can already see what is being described and match a verbal description to what is seen. In most instructional task materials, the listener typically has no version of what is being described and consequently starts with less initial information. This relative absence of listener knowledge creates a greater demand for explicitness on the speaker's part.

It is, of course, possible to devise versions of all instructional task materials in which this demand for explicitness is lesser or greater. For example, partially complete versions (of something to be completed via instructions) already contain fixed reference points that increase the shared knowledge, or common ground, for speaker and listener. This should normally make the communication of further referential information less demanding than in a task where little or no common ground is initially available. Keeping in mind that substantial variation, in terms of relative common ground, can be designed into instructional task materials, we consider three general types. These can be distinguished simply as drawing, tracing a route, and assembling.

Drawing

The most basic instructional task materials need only involve pencil and paper. The speaker, looking at a simple drawing on a piece of paper, gives instructions to a listener on how to draw the same thing. If the listener is given different colored pens, then the drawing can incorporate color. An arrangement of simple geometric shapes, as illustrated in Fig. 4.11, is easy to create and to vary. The simplicity of this task type allows it to be used in any context, regardless of available equipment or any other materials. The shapes to be drawn can be many or few and vary in size, color, and distance from each other. They can even be the creation of the participants, as in Pica et al. (1989).

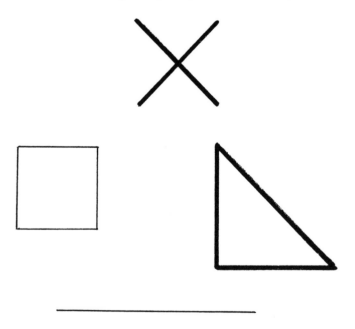

FIG. 4.11. Diagram.

Although there seem to be some prototypical form characteristics of squares and circles (Rosch, 1974), it is not necessary that the shapes to be drawn should be geometric. The shapes can range from simple doodles, as used in "the Squiggle Game" (Hawkins, 1985) to the more conventional (i.e., nameable) forms shown in Fig. 4.12. Research applications of the types of drawing task materials shown in Fig. 4.11 can be found in Brown and Yule (1983) and Yule (1981), and of those shown in Fig. 4.12, in Kellerman et al. (1990) and Russell (1997). Many other researchers (e.g., Gass & Varonis, 1985a; Oliver, 1995) reported on the use of picture-drawing tasks, but did not always include illustrations of the actual materials used.

Tracing a Route

For some participants, the apparent requirement of a drawing task (i.e., an ability to draw) creates a certain amount of apprehension and, occasionally, an expressed unwillingness to participate. Much less demanding in this regard (though perhaps only

FIG. 4.12. Shapes.

in terms of the drawing aspect) are those tasks where the listener has to draw a line on a map, tracing a route described by the speaker. In its simplest form, such a task may consist of a grid of city streets, conventionally labeled, with a straightforward path marked through them on the speaker's version. Or the route is marked on a larger scale map of a country and a journey has to be traced. The listener has an identical map, without the route. This is the basic design found in many pedagogical materials, particularly those used in the teaching of listening (cf. Geddes, 1981; Morley, 1984; Underwood, 1989).

In the versions used for referential communication research, there are typically more complexities. Incorporating the requirement of identifying one referent from an array of similar non-referents, Lloyd (1990, 1991, 1992) employed the route-finding materials shown as Fig. 4.13. This version shows the route to be communicated. Not shown in Fig. 4.13 are the color differences between many of the locations (e.g., different colored roofs on some buildings). This material, although bearing no resemblance to a genuine street map, does incorporate some of the kinds of referential problems found in other descriptive tasks, such as "Spot the difference."

Different versions of route-tracing materials have had more recognizable maplike qualities. One has an island containing a number of dangerous areas and a safe route marked on the speaker's version. As shown in Fig. 4.14A, 4.14B (from Anderson et al., 1991), the island map task has typically incorporated some differences between the two versions provided to the speaker (4.14A) and the listener (4.14B). In an early version, one of the maps was presented as having been "made by an earlier explorer" (Brown et al., 1984, p. 70) and consequently contained differences from the newer version. Some pedagogical uses of the island map task are explored in Anderson and Lynch (1988) and Rost (1990). Research applications are reported in Anderson (1995), Anderson et al. (1991), Brown (1986, 1987), and Brown et al. (1984).

The city map format, as shown in Fig. 4.15A, 4.15B, can also incorporate differences between the speaker's (4.15A) and lis-

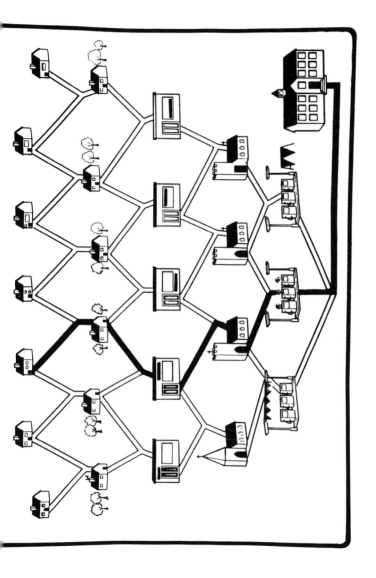

FIG. 4.13. Trace the route.

55

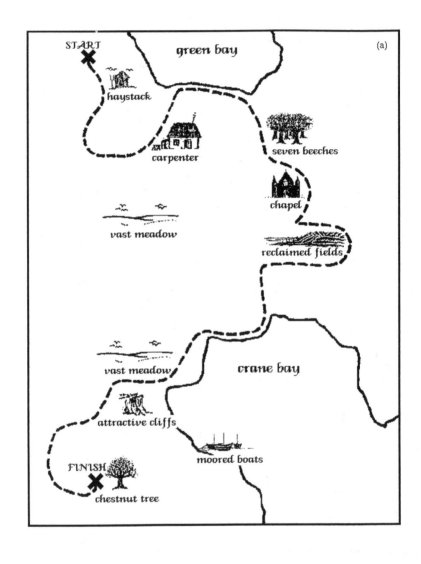

FIG. 4.14A. Island map (speaker's).

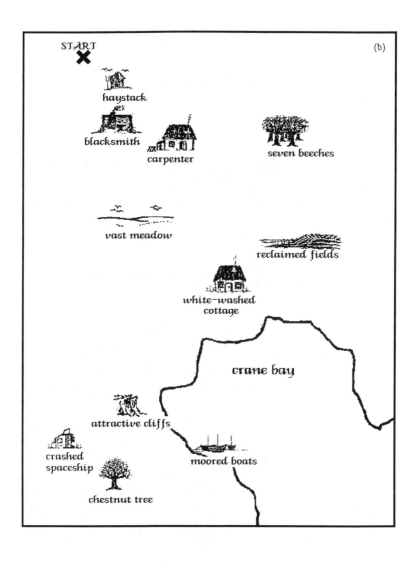

START

haystack

blacksmith

carpenter

seven beeches

vast meadow

reclaimed fields

white-washed cottage

crane bay

attractive cliffs

crashed spaceship

moored boats

chestnut tree

(b)

FIG. 4.14B. Island map (listener's).

tener's (4.15B) versions. Containing "a delivery route to ten locations" (Yule, 1990a, p. 54), the speaker's map differs from the listener's at four major points. For example, one location identified as a Hats store in Fig. 4.15A has become a Bicycles store in Fig. 4.15B. An area with a single Office in Fig. 4.15A has three Office buildings in Fig. 4.15B. The range of possible variations between the two map versions is actually unlimited.

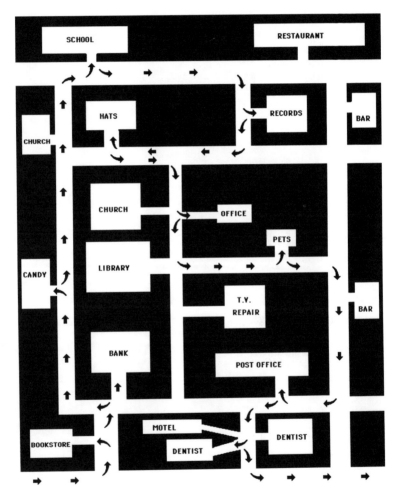

FIG. 4.15A. Map task (speaker's).

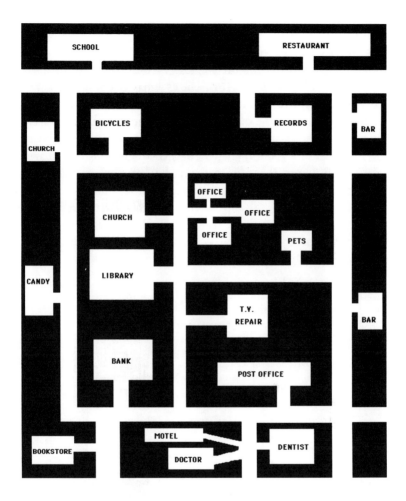

FIG. 4.15B. Map task (listener's).

The main reason given for including such differences is to create referential conflicts (Yule, 1991) in order to discover how those conflicts are resolved by L2 speakers. In most of this research, the participants are told at the beginning that they will encounter differences in their two versions of the map. An exception to this is found in Blakar (1984), where a number of map task studies are reported. In these studies, participants were given no warning that there would be differences between their maps.

One other variation on the basic route-tracing format is illustrated in Fig. 4.16A, 4.16B. The essential features of the map task materials are incorporated into a flow diagram, vaguely resembling some type of technical design (flow chart or circuit diagram). Once again, the route (or direction of flow) is marked on the speaker's version (Fig. 4.16A) through a number of areas and components that differ from the listener's version. For example, where Fig. 4.16A has a small component called J-2 and only one T. R. S. unit, Fig. 4.16B has that small component replaced by K-4 and there are three T. R. S. units. A research application of this material is reported in Yule, Powers, and Macdonald (1992).

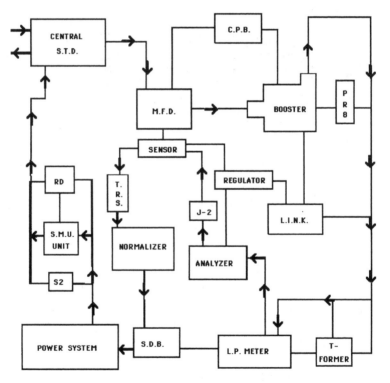

FIG. 4.16A. Flow diagram (speaker's).

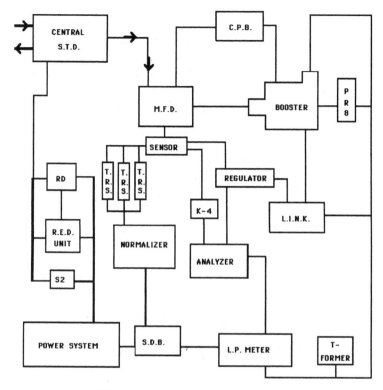

FIG. 4.16B. Flow diagram (listener's).

The instructional aspect of the task in tracing a route appears to be generally less troublesome than the identification of referent aspect. Indeed, such task materials create points at which the negotiation of reference is required. In tasks that require more assembly, it is the instructional language that needs to be even more explicit.

Assembling

In an assembly task, the speaker knows how the various parts of some object or design go together and has to instruct the listener to physically assemble those parts (often with the help of a drawing or photograph). A wide range of different materials have been employed in such tasks. Brown and Yule (1983) elicited instructions from speakers who were first shown how the different parts of a meat grinder (or mincer) went together and then asked to explain the assembly to a listener holding the disassembled parts. Other real-world objects that have featured in such tasks include an electrical plug, a tent, a chemical apparatus, a stapler, a caulking gun, a Christmas tree stand, and a Melior (or plunge) coffee pot. These last two are illustrated in Tarone and Yule (1989). In their tasks, a set of photographs of the assembly in progress (plus some that were not) were given to listeners so that they could identify which of the photographs matched the assembly instructions of the speaker. The speaker first watched the assembly being demonstrated on a (silent) videotape, then provided the instructions. Other research applications of this material are reported in Tarone (1986), Tarone and Yule (1987), and Yule and Tarone (1990).

Less demanding in terms of physical material and equipment are versions of the assembly task that use simple toys or designs. For example, in a "Plant the garden" task, speakers have felt boards and a number of felt shapes representing flowers. Speakers begin with a different group of shapes already on each of their boards and a set of loose shapes. They have to tell each other how to assemble their gardens and try to match a hidden master garden plot. An illustration of the materials used in this assembly task and research results are reported in Doughty and Pica (1986), with a variation called "Arrange the houses" also used in Pica et al. (1989) and Pica, Holliday, Lewis, Berducci, and Newman (1991). A similar type of exercise, incorporating the kind of referential problems found in description tasks, involves cutouts of plants, animals, and humans, sharing some attributes like color and size, which have to be placed in slots on a board (cf. Pica, Young, & Doughty, 1987). Similar materials involving a beach scene and a farm scene have been used by Gass and Varonis (1994). Using cardboard cutouts of a number of objects (and distractors) representing parts of a Christmas scene picture, Bialystok (1983) recorded instructions on how to reconstruct the picture on a large flannelboard. Lloyd, Boada, and Forns (1992) and Oliver (1995) used outlines of a kitchen with cutouts of items to be placed in the kitchen. Schober (1995) created a round board game with various shapes in different colors that looked like "a large pizza with strange toppings" (p. 230).

Another similar type of instructional task design employs a small pegboard, colored pegs, and colored rubber (or elastic) bands. The speaker has a diagram showing a particular arrangement of the pegs in the pegboard, with rubber bands stretched around some pegs, and instructs the listener which pegs and bands to choose and how to arrange them. Research applications are presented in Anderson, Yule, and Brown (1984) and Brown et al. (1984), which also contains illustrations of the design.

Block-building tasks fall into this same category. Scarcella and Higa (1981) used plastic colored blocks, to be assembled from instructions based on a picture, and Carroll and von Stutterheim (1993) reported on the use of an L-shaped figure made out of colored wooden blocks held together with screws, to be assembled from instructions. A wooden pyramid consisting of 21 interlocking pieces has featured in a number of research projects (e.g., Jamieson, 1994; Jamieson & Pedersen, 1993; Wood, Bruner, & Ross, 1976). More specifically, the toy construction materials known as Lego present opportunities for a wide range of assembly tasks (cf. Ur, 1988). The small blocks and flat pieces can be drawn or photographed in multiple configurations, providing assembly guidelines for speakers as they instruct hearers on how to replicate the structures. Those structures can be simple or complex, involving one or several colors, include human figures in identifiable shapes (e.g., boats, cars, planes), or simply represent arbitrary shapes. The version illustrated in Fig. 4.17 came from one small kit containing some preshaped parts and represents the type of material that has been used in a number of unpublished research applications. Published reports include Berwick (1993), Crookes (1989), Loschky and Bley-Vroman (1993), and Wagner (1983).

There are many other types of materials that can be used for instructional tasks. The typical requirement is simply that the features of the objects, drawings, or designs being used should

FIG. 4.17. Lego.

elicit referential communication and, if possible, allow the creation of different versions of the referential task. Although less easily controlled, tasks that require one speaker to demonstrate something (with instructions) to another have also featured in L2 research. In a "stage directions" task (Perdue, 1993), one participant watches a silent performance of a scene (e.g., missing the train), then has to direct another in a replay of the scene. In a different type of domain, Woken and Swales (1989) reported on a task where an expert instructs a novice on how to use a particular type of word processing program on a personal computer. Wright and Hull (1990) had one participant instruct another on how to make changes on a typescript.

ACCOUNTS OF INCIDENTS AND STORIES

Although many instructional tasks require the speaker to identify elements, keep them distinct, and put them in appropriate sequence, such demands are much more likely to be present in tasks that elicit narrative accounts. As Brown et al. (1984) pointed out, the elements in most descriptive and instructional tasks remain in static relationships. They typically do not change location, status, or appearance as the task proceeds. In contrast, such changes are normal in stories or any accounts of characters and events in time that incorporate dynamic relationships.

The use of cartoon strip drawings or photographs is very widespread in L2 teaching and research and needs very little explanation. Formats specific to referential communication usually involve not only the visual event sequence (for the speaker), but also a set of drawings or photographs to be identified by the hearer. Simple stories tend to have a single central character, only a small number of other characters, and relatively few changes in time and place. The dog and raven cartoon illustrated in Dechert (1983) is one example. Materials become more complex as the events depicted involve more shifts of main active character, more characters, more changes in location, and more background information or elements presented out of sequence. All these features create problems of reference, particularly problems in the maintenance of reference. For most people, telling a personal anecdote to a friend is not a difficult task, but recounting a series of observed incidents, explicitly keeping characters and locations distinct, can be problematic.

Eyewitness Accounts

One type of account with obvious real-world correlates, in terms of the need for clarity and referential explicitness, is the kind that would be required from a witness to an incident such as an accident or a crime. Loftus (1979) developed a number of scenarios as part of her research on the reliability of eyewitness testimony. Brown et al. (1984) reported on the use of a videotape depicting a thief at work in a crowd (obtained from a police crime prevention series) where the speaker had to report precisely what had been witnessed after viewing the short video. Brown (1989) reported on the use of videotaped scenes where different participants see different parts of the events. The beneficial realism of such material is offset by its lack of flexibility (i.e., the researcher cannot add, change, or remove any of the elements depicted).

In contrast, a set of photographs depicting various points during a car crash (created via toy cars and a replica of an intersection) could be easily modified to include more or fewer vehicles, similar or dissimilar types and colors of vehicles, and more or less complex crashes. Illustrations of such material and discussions of research applications can be found in Brown et al. (1984), Brown and Yule (1983), and Yule, Anderson, and Brown (1984). An alternative, reported in Bekerian and Dennett (1990), is to use a set of slides (depicting an auto–pedestrian accident), each slide being shown for 3 seconds.

Stories

It is much more common for cartoon strip sequences involving humans to be used in eliciting narratives. Fig. 4.18A is an illustration of a series of events in a grocery store that, in essence, puts the viewer in an eyewitness role. This format typically elicits conventional storytelling routines from native speakers (e.g., creating proper names for the store and/or the main character). Designed into this version is a major referential problem concerning where the bottle is placed by the child. Other versions can include drawings where all characters are same gender, creating a requirement for more explicit referring expressions. In the listener's version, Fig. 4.18B, the listener is given a set of jumbled individual scenes and asked to put them in order, following the speaker's account. An additional task is to require the listener to identify which scenes do not belong in the story, as told.

With a different plot, the narrative materials in Fig. 4.19A and 4.19B are also designed to elicit referential communication. Built into this narrative (Fig. 4.19A) are several changes of location

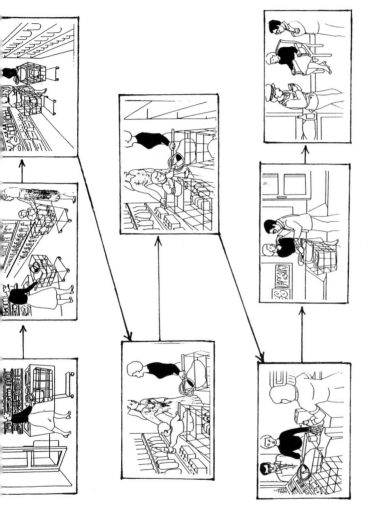

FIG. 4.18A. The supermarket (speaker's).

FIG. 4.18B. The supermarket (listener's).

that require explicit reference in the speaker's account. The listener's materials (Fig. 4.19B) have a number of scenes to be identified as part of the story, as told (or not), and ordered appropriately. These two narratives, called "The Supermarket" and "The Disco" have been used in an extremely large number of (unpublished) research projects. Some research applications have been reported in Brown et al. (1984), and Brown and Yule (1983).

A similar format has been used with videotaped (staged) events in a classroom setting and a set of still photographs. A significant feature of this research was the involvement of students in creating the materials. In the communication task, the speaker watches the videotape then tells the story. The listener has to select only those photographs (from a set of six) that fit

FIG. 4.19A. The disco (speaker's).

FIG. 4.19B. The disco (listener's).

the story, as told. Illustrations of this material and reports on research applications can be found in Tarone and Yule (1989). Other research findings are presented in Tarone (1989) and Tarone and Yule (1987).

An interesting use of existing film material (Charlie Chaplin's *Modern Times*) is reported in Perdue (1993). The speaker and researcher watch one episode from the film together, then the researcher leaves for the duration of a second episode and, on returning, has to be told what happened. This format has the advantage of creating an initial shared world of reference for both participants. Research applications of this material are reported in Dietrich (1989), Giacomi and Vion (1986), Huebner (1989), and Véronique (1990).

OPINIONS, PROBLEMS, AND DECISIONS

In task-based studies, many other communication exercises have been used for L2 research, but most of them have not been specifically designed for the investigation of referential communication. Although certainly incorporating the need for referential communication skills, tasks that are defined as opinion expressing, problem solving, or decision making are typically designed with a different type of primary focus. Prompted mainly by an interest in certain types of interactive language use, the design of such tasks typically involves substantial amounts of written information to be read, interpreted, and discussed. Answers or solutions then have to be negotiated. In many cases, they elicit the discussion of what Brown et al. (1984) characterized as abstract relationships (i.e., talk or argument in support of different opinions or positions).

In different tasks, opinions have been elicited on issues such as corporal punishment (Brown et al., 1984), the influence of television (Duff, 1986), the American revolution (Rulon & McCreary, 1986), and even the benefits (or not) of communication tasks in language learning (Pica et al., 1989). Professional work contexts as more real-world sites for such tasks are considered in Byrne and Fitzgerald (1994) and Willing (1992).

In what are often called problem-solving or decision-making tasks, a specific situation is created, with a limited set of options, and speakers are asked to make a decision. For example, you and others are on a sinking ship, each with a list of items, but only a small number of those items can be taken, so decisions have to be negotiated over which (and whose) items are important. This "Desert island" task was used in research reported by Duff (1986). Or you are in charge of deciding the new layout for a zoo, given a particular set of options and requirements, as reported in Newton (1995). Other examples are the "Heart transplant" decision (choose only one from six individuals who can receive a heart transplant), found in Newton (1995) and Pica and Doughty (1985a, 1985b), the "Nuclear war" task (select only 6 from 10 individuals who can board a plane to safety), reported in Plough and Gass (1993), and the "Plane crash" exercise (rank 10 individuals as survivors), used in Porter (1986). Such materials are frequently found in commercial L2 course-books and even form the content of whole texts (e.g., Rooks, 1981, 1983; Ur, 1981), along with puzzles and games (cf. Danesi, 1987; Omaggio, 1982; Palmer & Rodgers, 1983).

For some of the materials described in this section there are obvious activities to be undertaken. However, for others, there are several different procedures possible. In the next section, we review some of the procedures that have been favored by re-searchers.

PROCEDURES

Although there is a general information transmission require-ment determining the basic structure of referential communica-tion tasks, some variation in procedures can be found. By and large, the procedures are described for a pair of participants.

A Pair, A Table, and A Screen

The original experimental situation for two participants in a basic referential communication task, as described by Glucksberg and Krauss (1967), is reproduced as Fig. 4.20. Both participants are seated at a table, separated by an opaque screen. They both have the same six blocks and each block has an abstract design (from the set shown in Fig. 4.8). The speaker's six designs are prearranged in a certain order, but the listener's are not. The speaker's task is to describe each of the six abstract designs in sequence so that, by the end, the listener's set matches the speaker's. This basic experimental format is reported to present few practical problems for adults or "children as young as 36 months" (Glucksberg & Krauss, 1967, p. 310).

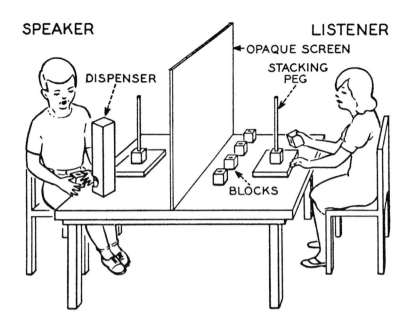

FIG. 4.20. A pair, a table, and a screen.

For young children, the task was presented as a game called "Stack the Blocks" and involved a pretraining session with pictures of animals on the blocks. Once the participants demonstrated an ability to follow the task procedure with the animal picture blocks, they were given the blocks with abstract designs. In essence, this pretraining activity obviated the need for lengthy verbal instructions and "greatly simplified teaching the rules and goal of the game" (Krauss & Glucksberg, 1969, p. 258). Unless the aim of the research is to discover a difference between performance with pretask preparation and without (cf. Crookes, 1989; Plough & Gass, 1993), participants in referential communication tasks are typically given an opportunity to become familiar with the type of materials and procedures prior to the performance(s) that will be recorded for research purposes.

The basic configuration of a speaker-director talking to a listener–matcher, separated by an opaque screen, has been replicated in many other studies in first (e.g., Clark & Wilkes-

Gibbs, 1986) and L2 (e.g., Bongaerts, Kellerman, & Bentlage, 1987) use.

With or Without a Barrier

For some researchers (e.g., Brown & Yule, 1983; Tarone & Yule, 1989), it is important that the screen or barrier used should allow participants to see each other's faces, while shielding the task materials from view. In one report expressing a similar motivation, the specific height of the screen was reported (40 centimeters, in Oliver, 1995).

A number of modifications to this basic configuration have been reported. In their "Plant the Garden" task, Doughty and Pica (1986) provided their speakers with separate boards and prevented them from viewing each other's materials by stipulating that "all work had to be carried out by each participant behind the board, which was held in a semi-vertical position" (p. 311). In some of the map task research (e.g., Yule, 1991), participants were given their different maps inside manila folders and instructed to avoid letting the other see their maps, thus eliminating the need for both barrier and table. Anderson et al. (1991) placed their maps on two drawing boards that were arranged back-to-back, concealing each map from the other's view, yet allowing eye contact. They then could add a barrier to create a "no eye contact" condition, for research purposes. The major determining factor in whether a barrier is used or some other format is adopted seems to be simply the amount of space required for the task materials.

With or Without a Listener

A crucial component in the original research design (see Fig. 4.20) was the presence of a listener to perform the matching task as the speaker spoke. An early distinction was made, however, between what Krauss and Weinheimer (1967) called the monologue condition (without a listener) and the dialogue condition (with listener present).

The Monologue Condition. The defining aspect of the monologue condition is the absence of an immediate listener. Basically, the speaker is asked to talk to a microphone or cassette recorder. A number of positive motivations for this design feature have been presented. Explicitly adopting a procedure already chosen by Jewson, Sachs, and Rohner (1981), Simons and Murphy (1986) asked children to "describe each of nine abstract figures into a tape recorder ... in order to make the language requirements of the task as similar as possible to a written language task" (p. 197). In essence, this aspect of the procedure is intentionally designed to elicit language that is not dependent on the immediate situation, but fits one in which "sender and receiver are separated in space and time" (Simons & Murphy, 1986, p. 197). In her research with children, Snow (1987) characterized this situation (no listener present) as "de-contextualized" in contrast to one with a live task partner that is "contextualized" (p. 12). Elsewhere, it is characterized as "distanced communication" (Rodino & Snow, 1997).

This isolation of the speaker may also be perceived as having positive value if any possible effects from the listener's participation have to be avoided. For example, in assessment uses of tasks, there may be a strong preference for only the speaker's performance (unaided, uninterrupted) to be recorded. One further practical motivation is numerical: Having a listener present (vs. a recorder) usually doubles the required number of participants.

The instructions to a speaker in the monologue condition generally mention a future listener who will have to perform some task. In some cases, there is reference to a hypothetical listener (Kellerman, Bongaerts, & Poulisse, 1987). It should be noted that the monologue condition does present a subtle kind of demand on the speaker to invent a listener rather than to recognize a listener (as in the dialogue condition) and an assumption that everyone will invent the same type of listener. It is also clear that the monologue condition allows for none of the collaboration or negotiation aspects considered important in some referential communication studies.

The Dialogue Condition.   In perhaps the simplest version of
the original dialogue condition, one participant had four color
chips, numbered 1 through 4, whereas the other participant had
the same four chips, arranged in a different order, lettered A
through D. Their task was to arrive at number–letter matchings,
while "visually separated" (Krauss & Weinheimer, 1967, p. 360).
The two participants in the original research were similar in
profile (e.g., age, proficiency, status, ethnicity).

Whereas the monologue condition creates a uniformly zero-
feedback effect, the dialogue condition can have a range of
different feedback effects. The instructions to the participants
can be used to impose a zero-feedback restriction or a limited
feedback role on the listener. In one version of limited feedback,
the participants perform the task face-to-face, but the listener
may only provide nonverbal feedback (head nods, puzzled
looks) to the speaker, as described in Tarone and Yule (1987). In
an encouraged-feedback role, the listener may be told to provide
verbal feedback at any point during task performance, but the
task itself is not designed to require that feedback. In one highly
structured version of this type of feedback condition, the listener (receiver) "was required to press a buzzer to indicate that
she wanted to question the sender" (Alkire, Collum, Kaswan, &
Love, 1968, p. 303). In a required-feedback version, the listener
has crucial information needed for the completion of the task
(as designed) and has to respond to the speaker. This is also
known as a jigsaw type of arrangement (cf. Pica, Kanagy, &
Falodun, 1993).

The listener role in most dialogue conditions is taken by
another naïve participant, generally another student. (See the
discussion of participant roles in chapter 3.) However, in some
investigations, that role is taken by the researcher, for example,
in Bialystok (1983), Pechman and Deutsch (1982), and Robinson (1995). Convenient though this may be, it does create a
rather special dyad. As has been emphasized by sociolinguists,
the nature of the addressee or audience has a powerful impact
on the language and style of the speaker (cf. Bell, 1984). Consequently, the unique status of the researcher (clearly knowledge-

able about the task materials already) may have a profound effect on communicative task performance.

In most dialogue conditions, the participants are seated face-to-face, but they are sometimes positioned side-by-side (e.g., Snow, 1987), or back-to-back (e.g., Berwick, 1993; Clennell, 1995). In one study, Boyle, Anderson, and Newlands (1994) actually compared performances in the dialogue condition when participants could, and could not, see each other, concluding that visibility improves information transfer. There has been criticism (e.g., Erickson, 1981) of the artificiality of any non-face-to-face task arrangements, but other researchers (e.g., Ellis & Beattie, 1986) have noted that (natural) human communication takes place in a wide range of different (real) conditions. In some task uses, the participants are placed in separate rooms and communicate via an intercom system (Krauss & Fussell, 1990) or via telephone (e.g., Lloyd, 1990), or the task itself requires the speaker to use the telephone to find some information (e.g., Varonis & Gass, 1985b). In some studies the difference between being a direct participant or listener and being an overhearer or eavesdropper has been investigated (cf. Clark & Schaeffer, 1987b; Kraut, Lewis, & Swezey, 1982; Schober & Clark, 1989). The direct participant has a big advantage.

The general conclusion from a consideration of materials and procedures is that any decision in this area can have an effect on the nature of task performance and it is important to think carefully about such decisions well in advance of data gathering. Having taken the plunge and gathered the data, the researcher then has to decide on a suitable analytic framework to focus the analysis of that data.

FURTHER READING

Visual materials of the type that have been used (or adapted) for referential communication tasks can be found in Hill (1960), Rinvolucri (1984), Rollet and Tremblay (1975), Smith and Hanson (1992), Thomsen (1994), Ur (1988), or Wright (1989). The original referential communication task materials are illustrated in Glucksberg and Krauss (1967) and reproduced in Poulisse

(1990). Both Brown and Yule (1983) and Tarone and Yule (1989) have appendices containing illustrations of their materials. In addition to the reports already mentioned in the chapter, different investigations have employed descriptive tasks, such as Deutsch, Bruhn, Masche, and Behrens (1997), Gardner (1987), Lightbown (1987), Linde and Labov (1975), Mangold and Pobel (1988), and Rinck, Williams, Bower, and Becker (1996). Others mentioning drawing or instructional tasks are Avery, Ehrlich, and Yorio (1985), Ehrlich, Avery, and Yorio (1989), Lloyd (1997), Lloyd, Camaioni, and Ercolani (1995), Perdue (1993), Riesbeck (1980), Shortreed (1993), Snow (1987), and Yule (1982). Other eyewitness account studies include Bekerian and Bowers (1983), Bowers and Bekerian (1984), Brown (1989), and Geiselman, Fisher, MacKinnon, and Holand (1986), with Edwards and Middleton (1986) as an interesting study of how such accounts can be co-constructed. Two good resources on the analysis of storytelling tasks are Bamberg (1987) and Chafe (1980). Among the many studies employing narrative tasks are Derwing (1989), Ellis (1987a), Hulstijn and Hulstijn (1984), Pica et al. (1996), Poulisse (1990), Robinson (1995), Tomlin (1984), Trévise (1987), and von Stutterheim and Klein (1989).

5
Analytic Frameworks

The original analytic framework for referential communication simply compared the noun phrases used to identify entities by speakers of different ages or on different occasions. This type of investigation continues to be undertaken, with particular interest in changes in the form of referring expressions used by a pair of speakers during repeated performances on the same task. For example, in performing the same identification task over five trials, the same participants identified an abstract shape initially with the expression *looks like an hourglass with legs on each side*, then with *hourglass with legs*, then *hourglass-shaped thing*, then on the final two trials, they simply said *hourglass* (Krauss, 1987, p. 94). Various measures of length of referring expression are plotted relative to number of trials (i.e., task performances) to show that familiarity creates shorter messages (cf. Isaacs & Clark, 1987; Krauss & Fussell, 1990). More comprehensive attempts to measure information content in task performance have also produced frameworks that quantify message completeness, allowing a comparison between more and less effective information transfer (cf. Brown et al., 1984; Brown & Yule, 1983).

In L2 studies, the analytic frameworks have been designed to capture more of what is typical of L2 discourse. We briefly survey frameworks used for analyzing communication strategies, negotiated meaning, and communicative outcomes.

COMMUNICATION STRATEGIES

Communication strategies are the means used to overcome some difficulty in expressing an intended message. Faced with a difficulty, the speaker can overcome the problem by not attempting to express the intended meaning (an avoidance or reduction strategy) or by finding some other way to express it (an achievement or compensatory strategy). Most interest has been in the different types of compensatory strategies. Previous research has been conducted from two different perspectives. In one, the important distinctions are in terms of cognitive processing and only a small number of category types are proposed. The emphasis is on psychological processes and not on referential expressions. In the other, the focus is on the wide range and variability of different expressions used as communication strategies, leading to a fairly large number of analytic categories. There is also an interest, in this approach, in identifying procedural or core vocabulary used for reference. We try to reconcile the two perspectives here, combining them in Table 5.1. For overviews of the different approaches, see Bialystok (1990), Kellerman (1991), Poulisse (1990), Yule and Tarone (1997), and the contributions in Faerch and Kasper (1983).

The cognitive processing perspective can be seen as a "higher order description" (Bialystok, 1990, p. 114) of category types that have their realizations at a lower level and can be described by a wider range of more specific labels. Given some perceived difficulty in attempting to refer to an entity, the speaker can adopt a strategy that is *conceptual* (focusing on the entity itself as a concept) or *code* (focusing on a linguistic form). A conceptual strategy is either *holistic* (using a term for a related substitute

TABLE 5.1

Communication Strategies

1. Achievement (Compensatory)
   a. Conceptual: Holistic: approximation (analogy, superordinate)
                  Analytic: circumlocution (characteristics, color, function, shape, size)
   b. Code: borrowing, foreignizing, word coinage
2. Reduction (Avoidance)
   topic avoidance, message replacement, message abandonment
3. Interactive
   mime, gesture, sound imitation, appeal for assistance

concept) or *analytic* (describing properties of the referent). The most common form of a holistic strategy is known as *approximation*, through which the speaker attempts to get the listener to recognize the referent by using an analogy (e.g., *is something like a rope*) or a more general term, such as a superordinate (e.g., *it's a kind of animal*). The most typical analytic strategy is known as *circumlocution*, in which the speaker includes details of the entity (color, material, parts, shape, size, etc.) or mentions its likely function (e.g., *the thing you use to open the wine*). By contrast, different code strategies are all tied to linguistic form, as when the speaker tries to take a word straight from the L1 and use it in the L2 (*borrowing* or *code-switching*), makes an L1 term sound like an L2 form (*foreignizing*) or even creates a completely new form or neologism (*word coinage*).

In what are known as avoidance or reduction strategies, the speaker may simply not say anything about some part of the message (*topic avoidance*), may change a part (*message replacement*), or may simply give up (*message abandonment*). If the listener is physically present, then some interactive strategies can be attempted, using mime, gesture, sound imitation, or even an *appeal for assistance* (e.g., *how do you say in English that word—we say in Spanish bujia?*).

This list of strategy labels is not exhaustive and many others have been used for specific types of data analysis (cf. Bialystok, 1990; Dörnyei, 1995; Poulisse, Bongaerts, & Kellerman, 1984; Tarone, 1981; Váradi, 1980). It is important to remember that the type of task, participants, materials, and procedures all have an effect on what kinds of strategies are used by speakers. Whereas communication strategy analysis originated in the language of the L2 speaker (the output), the analytic framework for negotiated meaning originated in the language addressed to the L2 speaker (the input).

NEGOTIATED MEANING

Unlike some of the data elicited for communication strategy research, the data for negotiated meaning studies has to involve at least a pair of speakers interacting together on a task. The type of negotiation has been defined in the following way: "Negotiation between learners and interlocutors takes place during the course of their interaction when either one signals with questions or comments that the other's preceding message has not been successfully conveyed. The other then responds, often by repeating or modifying the message" (Pica et al., 1996, p. 61). It is worth noting that only trouble spots in the elicited data are the subject of this analysis. The key properties of that data are indications of adjustments being made to modify the interaction in order to make it comprehensible. Those indications come within a structure that can be exemplified with the following example from Varonis and Gass (1985b, p. 79):

S: had to declare declare? her ingress   (Trigger)
J: English?   (Indicator)
S: No, English no (laugh) ... ingress, her ingress (Response)

In this example, one speaker refers to something (i.e., her income) that the other speaker is not sure she understands. In the analytic framework, the initial reference is the Trigger, the expression of uncertainty about that reference is the Indicator, followed by the Response.

Most research interest has focused on the different kinds of indicators (also known as signals, as in Pica et al., 1989), because they are considered to be crucial elements in letting speakers know that their messages are inadequate in some way. Basic types of indicators are sometimes categorized as clarification requests (e.g., *what?*, *huh?*, *pardon?*), repetition requests (e.g., *could you say that again?*, *what was that?*), confirmation checks (e.g., *did you say "broken"?*, *English?*), and comprehension checks (e.g., *okay?*, *understand?*). In earlier (L1) studies, these were all treated as different types of clarification request (as shown in Table 5.2). Indicators of this type lead participants into the negotiation of meaning. In many cases, that negotiation is not primarily about reference, but about the form of the utterance. Indeed, in some recent versions of this approach, the most important aspect of such negotiation is specifically identified as a focus on form (cf.

Lightbown & Spada, 1990; Long, 1991). In the following example (Yule, 1994, p. 190), the two NNS participants negotiate what is being said (i.e., the form), via two clarification requests, in order to arrive at the referential meaning:

NNS1: they fuck us on the meaning
NNS2: they what?   (= clarification request)
NNS1: they fock us on the meaning
NNS2: oh focus?   (= clarification request)
NNS1: yeah they focus on the meaning always

The changed form may be classified as a phonological modification (a sound), a lexical modification (a word), or a structural modification (a grammatical form). In the L1 research tradition, the indicators of uncertainty were treated as types of contingent query (Garvey, 1977), but the set of categories presented in Table 5.2 have all generally been treated as kinds of clarification request (cf. Garvey, 1979; Lloyd, 1992, 1993; McTear, 1985, 1987; Ochs, 1987).

It is worth noting, from a data analytic perspective, that in many transcripts of task performance, indicators will occur on one side of the page (i.e., Speaker A), and on the other side of the page (i.e., Speaker B), there are often communication strategies produced in response, but this pattern has never been fully investigated. As illustration, the following example from Pica (1987, p. 6), reconsidered in Yule and Tarone (1991, p. 166), involves an English NS as Speaker A and a NNS as Speaker B:

TABLE 5.2
Clarification Requests

(A: turn at the first join of the road)	
1. Repetition request (non-specific)	B: *what?*
2. Repetition request (specific)	B: *the first what?*
3. Confirmation request	B: *the first 'join'?*
4. Specification request	B: *which road?*
5. Elaboration request	B: *turn and go where?*

	Speaker A	*Speaker B*
1		and they have the chwach there
2	the what?	
3		the chwach—I know someone that—
4	what does it mean?	
5		like um like American people they always go there every Sunday
6	yes?	
7		you know—every morning that there pr—that—the American people get dressed up to go to um chwach
8	oh to church—I see	

Speaker A produces two clarification requests in turns 2 and 4, and Speaker B produces two examples of circumlocution in response (turns 5 and 7).

This brief review of aspects of the framework used to study the negotiation of meaning hardly matches the extremely large number of research reports on this topic (cf. Pica 1987, 1994 for overviews, and the Further Reading section for more examples).

COMMUNICATIVE OUTCOMES

In referential communication studies, a distinction can be made between the negotiation of meaning framework (mostly concerned with the identification of what the speaker actually said) and a framework for the negotiation of communicative outcome (mostly concerned with how referential conflicts are resolved). The communicative outcomes framework applies to those situations where some problem of reference has been encountered by the participants (the sender and receiver) in a task. The three broad categories of outcomes are no problem, nonnegotiated solution, and negotiated solution, which are further subdivided, as shown in Table 5.3. An overview of this type of analytic framework, with illustrative examples, can be found in Yule and Powers (1994).

This third type of framework can be applied to data that has already been analyzed within the preceding two frameworks. In

TABLE 5.3
Communicative Outcomes

1. *No problem*: A referential problem exists but is not identified.

2. *Non-negotiated solutions*

  a. *Unacknowledged problem*: A problem is identified by the receiver, but not ackowledged by the sender.

  b. *Abandon responsibility*: A problem is acknowledged by the sender, but responsibility is not taken for solving it.

  c. *Arbitrary solution*: A problem is acknowledged by the sender who solves it arbitrarily, ignoring the receiver's contribution.

3. *Negotiated solutions*

  a. *Other-centered solution*: The sender tries to solve the problem based on the receiver's (and the sender's) perspective.

  b. *Self-centered solution*: The sender tries to solve the problem by making the receiver's perspective fit the sender's.

the following example from Pica et al. (1991, p. 367), the first two lines can be viewed as a Trigger and an Indicator, respectively, the third line as a Circumlocution, and the fifth line as an Abandon Responsibility type of nonnegotiated solution:

NS:	does the TV have antennas?
NNS:	terrace?
NS:	yes, like two things coming up in the back antennas? ah …
NNS:	eh …
NS:	ok, we'll pass

What this transcript does illustrate is that, in many L2 referential communication tasks, successful identification of referent is not always accomplished, even when communication strategies and indications of negotiated meaning are present. Another important point to note about the analysis of this small fragment of task-based interaction is that no single perspective can capture all that might be involved in the data elicited via a referential communication task.

That statement may, in fact, be an appropriate point with which to conclude this brief exploration of referential communication research. In the course of this survey, I have tried to present an introduction to some of the issues, materials, and analytic approaches that have emerged in recent years. I hope that this introduction provides a good beginning, an incentive to read some of the research reports cited in the original, a motivation to take part in continuing the research, and a realization that it is not only possible, but likely, that you will be able to do it much better.

FURTHER READING

The original framework for analyzing referential communication data can be found in Krauss and Glucksberg (1977). Studies of the changes in referring expressions over repeated trials can be found in Carroll (1980), Krauss (1987), Krauss and Fussell (1990), and Krauss and Weinheimer (1964). Frequent overspecification or redundancy in those expressions is noted in Mangold and Pobel (1988) and Pechman (1989), whereas clarity and economy are reported by Poulisse (1997). Attempts to quantify message completeness are illustrated in Brown and Yule (1983) and Yule (1981, 1982). A useful attempt to distinguish among types of information (as crucial, major, or minor) is presented in Derwing (1989). On communication strategies, there are two major monographs, Bialystok (1990) and Poulisse (1990), and two major collections, Faerch and Kasper (1983) and Kasper and Kellerman (1997). Sometimes discussed in terms of *strategic competence*, representative examples of communication strategy projects are presented in Bongaerts and Poulisse (1989), Chen (1990), DeKeyser (1989), Galván and Campbell (1979), Labarca and Khanji (1986), Paribakht (1985), Rost and Ross (1991), Scholfield (1987), Tarone (1977, 1980, 1984), Tarone and Yule (1987), Turian and Altenberg (1991), Willems (1987), and Yule and Tarone (1990). Other useful resources are Berry-Bravo (1993), Bygate (1987), Dörnyei and Thurrell (1991), Duff (1997), Faerch and Kasper (1984), Kellerman and Bialystok (1997), and Yule (1990b). On core and procedural vocabulary, see Carter (1987) and Widdowson (1983), respectively. On the input–output distinction, read Swain (1985, 1995).

There are a number of different terms for the type of research that focuses on negotiated meaning, including *conversational adjustments, discourse repair, interactional modifications*, and *modified interaction*. Overviews can be found in Chaudron (1988), Long (1981, 1983a, 1983b, 1983c), Long and Porter (1985), Pica (1987, 1991, 1994), Wesche (1994), and Young and Doughty (1987). Some critical observations have been provided by Aston (1986), Ellis (1992), Fiksdal (1990), Gardner (1987), Hawkins (1985), and Young (1989). More specific studies are reported in Doughty and Pica (1986), Gass and Varonis (1984, 1985a, 1985b, 1986, 1989), Pica (1988, 1992), Pica and Doughty (1985a, 1988), Pica et al. (1989, 1991, 1996), Pica, Young, and Doughty (1987), Porter (1986), and Varonis and Gass (1985a). On L1 approaches to clarification requests, see Garvey (1977, 1984), Lloyd (1992), and McTear (1985).

Calls for research on communicative outcomes can be found in Hatch (1983) and Young (1984). Specific studies are presented in Yule (1990a, 1991, 1994), Yule and Macdonald (1990), and Yule, Powers, and Macdonald (1992). Related investigations, mainly from the perspective of social psychology, are presented in Blakar (1984, 1985), Clark (1992), Ochs (1987), Rommetveit (1974), and Rommetveit and Blakar (1979). Many researchers create adapted versions of analytic frameworks in order to capture specific aspects of the data elicited by the use of a task in a particular context. You should anticipate having to do the same. Two clearly presented examples of such frameworks (with categories and illustrations) can be found in Berwick (1993) and Pica (1992).

References

Ackerman, B. (1981a). Performative bias in children's interpretations of ambiguous referential communications. *Child Development, 52,* 1224–1230.

Ackerman, B. (1981b). The understanding of young children and adults of the deictic adequacy of communications. *Journal of Experimental Child Psychology, 31,* 256–270.

Alkire, A., Collum, M., Kaswan, J., & Love, L. (1968). Information exchange and accuracy of verbal communication under social power conditions. *Journal of Personality and Social Psychology, 9,* 301–308.

Alvy, K. (1968). Relation of age to children's egocentric and cooperative communication. *Journal of Genetic Psychology, 112,* 275–286.

Anderson, A. (1995). Negotiating coherence in dialogue. In M. Gernsbacher & T. Givón (Eds.), *Coherence in spontaneous text* (pp. 1–40). Amsterdam: John Benjamins.

Anderson, A., Bader, M., Bard, E., Boyle, E., Doherty, G., Garrod, S., Isard, S., Kowtko, J., MacAllister, J., Miller, J., Sotillo, C., Thompson, H., & Weinert, R. (1991). The HCRC map task corpus. *Language and Speech, 34,* 351–366.

Anderson, A., Clark, A., & Mullin, J. (1991). Introducing information in dialogues: Forms of introduction chosen by young speakers and responses elicited from young listeners. *Journal of Child Language, 18,* 663–687.

Anderson, A., Clark, A., & Mullin, J. (1994). Interactive communication between children: Learning how to make language work in dialogue. *Journal of Child Language, 21,* 439–463.

Anderson, A., & Lynch, T. (1988). *Listening.* Oxford, England: Oxford University Press.

Anderson, A., Yule, G., & Brown, G., (1984). Hearer-effects on speaker performance. *First Language, 5,* 23–40.

Asher, S. (1976). Children's ability to appraise their own and another person's communication performance. *Developmental Psychology, 12,* 24–32.

Asher, S. (1979). Referential communication. In G. Whitehurst & B. Zimmerman (Eds.), *The functions of language and cognition* (pp. 175–197). New York: Academic.

Asher, S., & Oden, S. (1976). Children's failure to communicate: An assessment of comparison and egocentrism explanations. *Developmental Psychology, 12,* 132–139.

Asher, S., & Parke, R. (1975). Influence of sampling and comparison processes on the development of communication effectiveness. *Journal of Educational Psychology, 67,* 64–75.

Asher, S., & Wigfield, A. (1981). Training referential communication skills. In W. Dickson (Ed.), *Children's oral communication skills* (pp. 105–126). New York: Academic Press.

Aston, G. (1986). Trouble-shooting in interaction with learners: The more the merrier. *Applied Linguistics, 7*, 128–143.

Aston, G. (1993). Notes on the interlanguage of comity. In G. Kasper & S. Blum-Kulka (Eds.), *Interlanguage pragmatics* (pp. 224–250). Oxford, England: Oxford University Press.

Atkinson, M., & Heritage, J. (1984). *Structures of social action. Studies in conversation analysis.* Cambridge, England: Cambridge University Press.

Avery, P., Ehrlich, S., & Yorio, C. (1985). Prosodic domains in foreigner talk discourse. In S. Gass & C. Madden (Eds.), *Input in second language acquisition* (pp. 214–229). Rowley, MA: Newbury House.

Bachman, L., & Palmer, A. (1985). *Basic concerns in language test validation.* Reading, MA: Addison-Wesley.

Bamberg, M. (1987). *The acquisition of narratives: Learning to use language.* Berlin, Germany: Mouton.

Barsalou, L. (1983). Ad hoc categories. *Memory and Cognition, 11*, 211–227.

Barsalou, L. (1992). *Cognitive psychology.* Hillsdale, NJ: Lawrence Erlbaum Associates.

Bates, E., Bretherton, I., & Snyder, L. (1988). *From first words to grammar.* Cambridge, England: Cambridge University Press.

Bates, E., & MacWhinney, B. (1981). Second language acquisition from a functional perspective: Pragmatic, semantic and perceptual strategies. *Annals of the New York Academy of Sciences, 379*, 190–214.

Bates, E., & MacWhinney, B. (1982). A functionalist approach to grammar. In E. Wanner & L. Gleitman (Eds.), *Language acquisition: The state of the art* (pp. 167–214). New York: Academic.

Beal, C., & Flavell, J. (1982). Effect of increasing the salience of message ambiguities on kindergarteners' evaluations of communicative success and message adequacy. *Developmental Psychology, 18*, 43–48.

Bearison, D., & Cassell, T. (1975). Cognitive decentration and social codes: Communicative effectiveness of young children from differing family contexts. *Developmental Psychology, 11*, 29–36.

Bearison, D., & Levey, L. (1977). Children's comprehension of referential communication: Decoding ambiguous messages. *Child Development, 48*, 716–721.

Bekerian, D., & Bowers, J. (1983). Eyewitness testimony: Were we misled? *Journal of Experimental Psychology: Human Learning and Memory, 9*, 139–145.

Bekerian, D., & Dennett, J. (1990). Spoken and written recall of visual narratives. *Applied Cognitive Psychology, 4*, 175–187.

Bell, A. (1984). Language style as audience design. *Language in Society, 13*, 145–204.

Berry-Bravo, J. (1993). Teaching the art of circumlocution. *Hispania, 76*, 371–377.

Berwick, R. (1993). Towards an educational framework for teacher-led tasks. In G. Crookes & G. Gass (Eds.), *Tasks in a pedagogical context. Integrating theory and practice* (pp. 97–124). Clevedon, England: Multilingual Matters.

Bialystok, E. (1983). Some factors in the selection and implementation of communication strategies. In C. Faerch & G. Kasper (Eds.), *Strategies in interlanguage communicaiton* (pp. 100–118). London: Longman.

Bialystok, E. (1990). *Communication strategies.* Oxford, England: Blackwell.

Bishop, D., & Adams, C. (1991). What do referential communication tasks measure? A study of children with specific language impairment. *Applied Psycholinguistics, 12,* 199–215.

Blakar, R. (1984). *Communication: A social perspective on clinical issues.* Oslo, Norway: Universitetsforlaget.

Blakar, R. (1985). Towards a theory of communication in terms of preconditions: A conceptual framework and some empirical explorations. In H. Giles & R. St. Clair (Eds.), *Recent advances in language, communication and social psychology* (pp. 11–40). Hillsdale, NJ: Lawrence Erlbaum Associates.

Bloom, L. (1991). *Language development from two to three.* Cambridge, England: Cambridge University Press.

Bloom, L. (1993). *The Transition from infancy to language.* Cambridge, England: Cambridge University Press.

Blum-Kulka, S., House, J., & Kasper, G. (Eds.). (1989). *Cross-cultural pragmatics: Requests and apologies.* Norwood, NJ: Ablex.

Boden, M. (1979). *Piaget.* London: Fontana.

Bongaerts, T., Kellerman, E., & Bentlage, A. (1987). Perspective and proficiency in L2 referential communication. *Studies in Second Language Acquisition, 9,* 171–200.

Bongaerts, T., & Poulisse, N. (1989). Communication strategies in L1 and L2: Same or different? *Applied Linguistics, 10,* 253–268.

Bowers, J., & Bekerian, D. (1984). When will post-event information distort eyewitness testimony? *International Journal of Applied Psychology, 69,* 466–472.

Boyle, E., Anderson, A., & Newlands, A. (1994). The effects of visibility on dialogue and performance in a cooperative problem solving task. *Language and Speech, 37,* 1–20.

Bredart, S. (1984). Children's interpretation of referential ambiguities and pragmatic inference. *Journal of Child Language, 11,* 665–672.

Breen, M., & Candlin, C. (1980). The essentials of a communicative curriculum in language teaching. *Applied Linguistics, 1,* 89–112.

Brown, G. (1986). Investigating listening comprehension in context. *Applied Linguistics, 7,* 285–302.

Brown, G. (1987). Modelling discourse participants' knowledge. In J. Monaghan (Ed.), *Grammar in the construction of texts* (pp. 90–97). London, England: Francis Pinter.

Brown, G. (1989). Making sense: The interaction of linguistic expression and contextual information. *Applied Linguistics, 10,* 97–108.

Brown, G., Anderson, A., Shillcock, R., & Yule, G. (1984). *Teaching talk: Strategies for production and assessment.* Cambridge, England: Cambridge University Press.

Brown, G., & Yule, G. (1983). *Teaching the spoken language.* Cambridge, England: Cambridge University Press.

Brown, G. D., Sharkey, A., & Brown, G. (1987). Factors affecting the success of referential communication. *Journal of Psycholinguistic Research, 16,* 535–549.

Brown, J. (1988). *Understanding research in second language learning.* Cambridge, England: Cambridge University Press.

Brown, P., & Dell, G. (1987). Adapting production to comprehension: The explicit mention of instruments. *Cognitive Psychology, 19,* 441–472.

Brown, P., & Levinson, S. (1987). *Politeness.* Cambridge, England: Cambridge University Press.

Bruner, J. (1983). *Child's talk.* New York: Norton.

Bryant, P. (1982). *Piaget: Issues and experiments.* Leicester, England: British Psychological Society.

Bygate, M. (1987). *Speaking.* Oxford, England: Oxford University Press.

Byrne, M., & Fitzgerald, H. (1994). Intercultural communication and problem-solving skills: A training approach. *Prospect, 9,* 7–16.

Camaioni, L., & Ercolani, A. (1988). The role of comparison activity in the development of referential communication. *International Journal of Behavioural Development, 11,* 403–413.

Canale, M. (1988). The measurement of communicative competence. *Annual Review of Applied Linguistics, 8,* 67–84.

Canale, M., & Swain, M. (1980). Theoretical bases of communicative approaches to second language teaching and testing. *Applied Linguistics, 1,* 89–112.

Candlin, C., & Murphy, D. (Eds.). (1987). *Language learning tasks.* Englewood Cliffs, NJ: Prentice-Hall.

Carroll, J. (1980). Naming and describing in social communication. *Language and Speech, 23,* 309–322.

Carroll, M., & von Stutterheim, C. (1993). The representation of spatial configurations in English and German and the grammatical structure of locative and anaphoric expressions. *Linguistics, 31,* 1011–1041.

Carter, R. (1987). Is there a core vocabulary? *Applied Linguistics, 8,* 178–193.

Cazden, C. (1992). *Whole language plus: Essays on literacy in the United States and New Zealand.* New York: Teachers College Press.

Celce-Murcia, M., Dörnyei, Z., & Thurrell, S. (1995). Communicative competence: A pedagogically motivated model with content specifications. *Issues in Applied Linguistics, 6,* 5–35.

Chafe, W. (Ed.). (1980). *The pear stories.* Norwood, NJ: Ablex.

Channell, J. (1994). *Vague language.* Oxford, England: Oxford University Press.

Chaudron, C. (1988). *Second language classrooms.* Cambridge, England: Cambridge University Press.

Chen, S. Q. (1990). A study of communication strategies in interlanguage production by Chinese EFL learners. *Language Learning, 40,* 155–187.

Cherry, C. (1966). *On human communication.* Cambridge, MA.: MIT Press.

Chomsky, C. (1969). *The acquisition of syntax in children from 5-10.* Cambridge, MA.: MIT Press.

Cicourel, A. (1974). *Cognitive sociology.* New York: Free Press.

Clark, E. (1971). On the acquisition of the meaning of *before* and *after. Journal of Verbal Learning and Verbal Behavior, 10,* 266–275.

Clark, E. (1993). *The lexicon in acquisition*. Cambridge, England: Cambridge University Press.

Clark, H. (1992). *Arenas of language use*. Chicago: University of Chicago Press.

Clark, H., & Schaefer, E. (1987a). Collaborating on contributions to conversations. *Language and Cognitive Processes, 2*, 19–41.

Clark, H., & Schaefer, E. (1987b). Concealing one's meaning from overhearers. *Journal of Memory and Language, 26*, 209–225.

Clark, H., & Schaefer, E. (1989). Contributing to discourse. *Cognitive Science, 13*, 259–294.

Clark, H., & Wilkes-Gibbs, D. (1986). Referring as a collaborative process. *Cognition, 22*, 1–39.

Clennell, C. (1994). Investigating the use of communication strategies by adult second language learners: A case for trusting your own judgment in classroom research. *TESOL Journal, 4*, 32–35.

Clennell, C. (1995). Communication strategies of adult ESL learners: A discourse perspective. *Prospect, 10*, 4–20.

Clyne, M. (1994). *Inter-cultural communication at work*. Cambridge, England: Cambridge University Press.

Cooreman, A., & Kilborn, K. (1991). Functionalist linguistics: Discourse structure and language processing in second language acquisition. In T. Huebner & C. Ferguson (Eds.). *Crosscurrents in second language acquisition and linguistic theories* (pp. 195–224). Amsterdam: John Benjamins.

Cosgrove, J., & Patterson, C. (1977). Plans and the development of listener skills. *Developmental Psychology, 13*, 557–564.

Cox, M. (Ed.). (1980). *Are young children egocentric?* New York: St. Martin's Press.

Croft, W. (1995). Autonomy and functionalist linguistics. *Language, 71*, 490–532.

Crookes, G. (1986). *Task classification: a cross-disciplinary review* (Tech. Rep. No. 4). University of Hawaii, Honolulu: Center for Second Language Classroom Research.

Crookes, G. (1989). Planning and interlanguage variation. *Studies in Second Language Acquisition, 11*, 367–383.

Crookes, G., & Gass, S. (Eds.). (1993a). *Tasks and language learning. Integrating theory and practice*. Clevedon, England: Multilingual Matters.

Crookes, G., & Gass, S. (Eds.). (1993b). *Tasks in a pedagogical context. Integrating theory and practice*. Clevedon, England: Multilingual Matters.

Cumming, A. (1994). Alternatives in TESOL research: Descriptive, interpretive, and ideological orientations. *TESOL Quarterly, 28*, 673–703.

Danesi, M. (1987). The psychology and methodology of puzzles in L2 teaching. In J. Lantolf & A. Labarca (Eds.), *Research in second language learning: Focus on the classroom* (pp. 107–116). Norwood, NJ: Ablex.

Davies, N. (1982). Training fluency: An essential factor in language acquisition and use. *RELC Journal, 13*, 1–13.

Day, R. (Ed.). (1986). *Talking to learn: Conversation in second language acquisition*. Rowley, MA.: Newbury House.

Dechert, H. (1983). How a story is done in a second language. In C. Faerch & G. Kasper (Eds.), *Strategies in interlanguage communication* (pp. 175–195). London: Longman.

Deese, J. (1974). Towards a psychological theory of the meaning of sentences. In A. Silverstein (Ed.), *Human communication: Theoretical explorations.* (pp. 67–80). Hillsdale, NJ: Lawrence Erlbaum Associates.

DeKeyser, R. (1989). Communicative processes and strategies. *Annual Review of Applied Linguistics, 9,* 108–121.

Derwing, B. (1989). Information type and its relation to nonnative speaker comprehension. *Language Learning, 39,* 157–172.

Deutsch, W., Bruhn, N., Masche, G., & Behrens, H. (1997). Can one be more than two? Mono- and bilinguals' production of German and Spanish object descriptions in a referential communication task. In G. Kasper & E. Kellerman (Eds.), *Communication strategy research: Psycholinguistic and sociolinguistic aspects.* London: Longman.

Dickson, W. (Ed.). (1981). *Children's oral communication skills.* New York: Academic.

Dickson, W. (1982). Two decades of referential communication research: A review and meta-analysis. In C. Brainerd & M. Pressley (Eds.), *Verbal processes in children* (pp. 1–33). Berlin, Germany: Springer-Verlag.

Dietrich, R. (1989). Communicating with few words. An empirical account of the second language speaker's lexicon. In R. Dietrich & C. Graumann (Eds.), *Language processing in social context* (pp. 233–276). Amsterdam: Elsevier.

Dil, A. (Ed.). (1971). *Language in social groups.* Stanford, CA: Stanford University Press.

Dimbleby, R., & Burton, G. (1992). *More than words: An introduction to communication* (2nd ed.). London: Routledge.

Dines, E. (1980). Variation in discourse—and "stuff like that." *Language in Society, 9,* 13–31.

Donahue, M., Pearl, R., & Bryan, T. (1982). Learning disabled children's syntactic proficiency on a communication task. *Journal of Speech and Hearing Disorders, 47,* 397–403.

Donaldson, M. (1978). *Children's minds.* London: Fontana.

Dörnyei, Z. (1995). On the teachability of communication strategies. *TESOL Quarterly, 29,* 55–84.

Dörnyei, Z., & Thurrell, S. (1991). Strategic competence and how to teach it. *ELT Journal, 45,* 16–23.

Doughty, C., & Pica, T. (1986). "Information gap" tasks: Do they facilitate second language acquisition? *TESOL Quarterly, 20,* 305–325.

Duff, P. (1986). Another look at interlanguage talk: Taking task to task. In R. Day (Ed.). *Talking to learn: Conversation in second language acquisition* (pp. 147–181). Rowley, MA: Newbury House.

Duff, P. (1993). Tasks and interlanguage performance: An SLA research perspective. In G. Crookes & S. Gass (Eds.), *Tasks and language learning. Integrating theory and practice* (pp. 57–95). Clevedon, England: Multilingual Matters.

Duff, P. (1997). The lexical generation gap: A connectionist account of circumlocution in Chinese as a second language. In G. Kasper & E. Kellerman (Eds.), *Communication strategy research: Psycholinguistic and sociolinguistic aspects.* London: Longman.

Duran, R., Canale, M., Penfield, J., Stansfield, C., & Liskin-Gasparro, J. (1985). *TOEFL from a communicative viewpoint on language proficiency: A working paper.* (TOEFL Research Rep. 17). Princeton, NJ: Educational Testing Service.

Durkin, K. (1981). Aspects of late language acquisition: School children's use and comprehension of prepositions. *First Language, 3,* 47–59.

Durkin, K. (1986). Language and social cognition during the school years. In K. Durkin (Ed.), *Language development in the school years* (pp. 203–233). London: Croom Helm.

Edwards, D., & Middleton, D. (1986). Joint remembering: Constructing an account of shared experience through conversational discourse. *Discourse Processes, 9,* 423–459.

Ehrlich, S., Avery, P., & Yorio, C. (1989). Discourse structure and the negotiation of comprehensible input. *Studies in Second Language Acquisition, 11,* 397–414.

Eisenstein, M., Wolfson, N., Henning, G., & Chaudron, C. (1986). Alternatives in second language research: Three articles on the state of the art. *TESOL Quarterly, 20,* 683–717.

Elffers, J. (1976). *Tangram. The ancient Chinese shapes game.* New York: McGraw-Hill.

Ellis, A., & Beattie, G. (1986). *The psychology of language and communication.* Hillsdale, NJ: Lawrence Erlbaum Associates.

Ellis, N., & McClintock, A. (1994). *If you take my meaning. Theory into practice in human communication* (2nd ed.). London: Edward Arnold.

Ellis, R. (1985). *Understanding second language acquisition.* Oxford, England: Oxford University Press.

Ellis, R. (1987a). Interlanguage variability in narrative discourse: Style shifting in the use of the past tense. *Studies in Second Language Acquisition, 9,* 1–19.

Ellis, R. (Ed.). (1987b). *Second language acquisition in context.* Englewood Cliffs, NJ: Prentice-Hall.

Ellis, R. (1992). The classroom context: An acquisition-rich or an acquisition-poor environment? In C. Kramsch & McConnell-Ginet (Eds.), *Text and context* (pp. 171–186). Lexington, MA: Heath.

Ellis, R. (1994). *The study of second language acquisition.* Oxford, England: Oxford University Press.

Emerson, H., & Getkowski, W. (1980). Development of comprehension of sentences with "because" or "if." *Journal of Experimental Child Psychology, 29,* 202–204.

Erickson, F. (1981). Timing and context in everyday discourse: Implications for the study of referential and social meaning. In W. Dickson (Ed.), *Children's oral communication skills* (pp. 241–269). New York: Academic Press.

Faerch, C., & Kasper, G. (Eds.). (1983). *Strategies in interlanguage communication.* London: Longman.

Faerch, C., & Kasper, G. (1984). Two ways of defining communication strategies. *Language Learning, 34,* 45–63.

Fauconnier, G. (1994). *Mental spaces.* Cambridge, England: Cambridge University Press.

Fiksdal, S. (1989). Framing uncomfortable moments in crosscultural gatekeeping interviews. In S. Gass, C. Madden, D. Preston, & L. Selinker (Eds.), *Variation in second language acquisition. Volume 1. Discourse and pragmatics.* (pp. 190–207).

Fiksdal, S. (1990). *The right time and place: A microanalysis of cross-cultural gatekeeping interviews.* Newark, NJ: Ablex.

Flavell, J. (1981). Cognitive monitoring. In W. Dickson (Ed.), Children's oral communication skills (pp. 35–60). New York: Academic.

Flavell, J., Botkin, P., Fry, C., Wright, J., & Jarvis, P. (1968). *The development of role-taking and communication skills in children.* New York: Wiley.

Flavell, J., Miller, P., & Miller, S. (1993). *Cognitive development.* (3rd ed.). Englewood Cliffs, NJ: Prentice-Hall.

Flavell, J., & Ross, L. (1981). *Social cognitive development: Frontiers and possible futures.* Cambridge, England: Cambridge University Press.

Flavell, J., Speer, J., Green, F., & August, D. (1981). The development of comprehension monitoring and knowledge about communication. *Monographs of the Society for Research in Child Development* (No. 192).

Fletcher, P., & Garman, M. (Eds.). (1986). *Language Acquisition.* Cambridge, England: Cambridge University Press.

Foley, J. (1991). A psycholinguistic framework for task-based approaches to language teaching. *Applied Linguistics, 12,* 62–75.

Ford, W., & Olson, D. (1975). The elaboration of the noun phrase in children's description of objects. *Journal of Experimental Child Psychology, 19,* 371–382.

Franklin, M., & Barten, S. (Eds.) (1988). *Child language: A reader.* Oxford, England: Oxford University Press.

Frawley, W., & Lantolf, J. (1985). Second language discourse: A Vygotskyan perspective. *Applied Linguistics, 6,* 19–44.

Fry, C. (1966). Training children to communicate to listeners. *Child Development, 37,* 674–685.

Fussell, S., & Krauss, R. (1989). The effects of intended audience on message production and comprehension: Reference in a common ground framework. *Journal of Experimental Social Psychology, 25,* 203–219.

Gallaway, C., & Richards, B. (Eds.). (1994). *Input and interaction in language acquisition.* Cambridge, England: Cambridge University Press.

Galván, J., & Campbell, R. (1979). An examination of the communication strategies of two children in the Culver City Spanish immersion program. In R. Andersen (Ed.), *The acquisition and use of Spanish as first and second language.* (pp. 133–150). Washington, DC: TESOL.

Gardner, D. (1987). Communication games: Do we know what we're talking about? *ELT Journal, 41,* 19–24.

Garfinkel, H. (1967). *Studies in ethnomethodology.* Englewood Cliffs, NJ: Prentice-Hall.

Garmiza, C., & Anisfeld, M. (1976). Factors reducing the efficiency of referent communication in children. *Merrill-Palmer Quarterly of Behavior and Development, 22,* 125–136.

Garrod, S., & Anderson, A. (1987). Saying what you mean in dialogue: A study in conceptual and semantic co-ordination. *Cognition, 27,* 181–218.

Garvey, C. (1977). The contingent query: A dependent act in conversation. In M. Lewis & L. Rosenblum (Eds.), *Interaction, conversation and the devel-*

opment of language: The origin of behavior. (Vol. 5, pp. 63–94) New York: Wiley.

Garvey, C. (1979). Contingent queries and their relations in discourse. In E. Ochs & B. Schieffelin (Eds.), *Developmental pragmatics* (pp. 363–372). New York: Academic Press.

Garvey, C. (1984). *Children's talk.* Cambridge, MA: Harvard University Press.

Garvey, C., & Hogan, R. (1973). Social speech and social interaction: Egocentrism revisited. *Child Development, 44,* 562–568.

Gass, S., Cohen, A., & Tarone, E. (1994). Introduction. In E. Tarone, S. Gass, & A. Cohen (Eds.), *Research methodology in second language acquisition* (pp. xiii–xxiii). Hillsdale, NJ: Lawrence Erlbaum Associates.

Gass, S., Madden, C., Preston, D., & Selinker, L. (Eds.). (1989a). *Variation in second language acquisition: Vol. 1. Discourse and pragmatics.* Clevedon, England: Multilingual Matters.

Gass, S., Madden, C., Preston, D., & Selinker, L. (Eds.). (1989b). *Variation in second language acquisition: Vol. 2. Psycholinguistic issues.* Clevedon, England: Multilingual Matters.

Gass, S., & Selinker, L. (1994). *Second language acquisition.* Hillsdale, NJ: Lawrence Erlbaum Associates.

Gass, S., & Varonis, E. (1984). The effect of familiarity on the comprehensibility of non-native speech. *Language Learning, 34,* 65–89.

Gass, S., & Varonis, E. (1985a). Task variation and nonnative/nonnative negotiation of meaning. In S. Gass & C. Madden (Eds.), *Imput in second language acquisition* (pp. 149–161). Rowley, MA: Newbury House.

Gass, S., & Varonis, E. (1985b). Variation in native speaker speech modification to non-native speakers. *Studies in Second Language Acquisition, 7,* 37–58.

Gass, S., & Varonis, E. (1986) Sex differences in NNS/NNS negotiation of meaning. In R. Day (Ed.), *Talking to learn: Conversation in second language acquisition* (pp.327–351). Towley, MA: Newbury House.

Gass, S., & Varonis, E. (1989). Incorporated repairs in nonnative discourse. In M. Eisenstein (Ed.). *The dynamic interlanguage. Empirical studies in second language variation* (pp. 71–86). New York: Plenum.

Gass, S., & Varonis, E. (1994). Input, interaction and second language production. *Studies in Second Language Acquisition, 16,* 283–302.

Geddes, M. (1981). Listening. In K. Johnson & K. Morrow (Eds.), *Communication in the classroom* (pp. 78–86). London: Longman.

Geiselman, R., Fisher, R., MacKinnon, D., & Holland, H. (1986). Enhancement of eyewitness memory with the cognitive interview. *American Journal of Psychology, 99,* 385–401.

Giacomi, A., & Vion, R. (1986). Metadiscursive processes in the acquisition of a second language. *Studies in Second Language Acquisition, 8,* 355–368.

Ginsburg, H., & Opper, S. (1988). *Piaget's theory of intellectual development.* (3rd ed.). Englewood Cliffs, NJ: Prentice-Hall.

Givón, T. (1979). *On understanding grammar.* New York: Academic.

Givón, T. (1984). Universals of discourse structure and second language acquisition. In W. Rutherford (Ed.), *Language universals and second language acquisition* (pp. 109–136) Amsterdam: John Benjamins.

Givón, T. (1989). *Mind, code and context: Essays in pragmatics.* Hillsdale, NJ: Lawrence Erlbaum Associates.

Givón, T. (1995). *Functionalism and grammar.* Amsterdam: John Benjamins.

Glucksberg, S., & Krauss, R. (1967). What do people say after they have learned how to talk? Studies in the development of referential communication. *Merrill-Palmer Quarterly, 13,* 309–316.

Glucksberg, S., Krauss, R., & Higgins, E. (1975). The development of referential communication skills. In F. Horowitz (Ed.), *Review of child development research.* (Vol. 4, pp. 305–345). Chicago: University of Chicago Press.

Glucksberg, S., Krauss, R., & Weisberg, R. (1966). Referential communication in nursery school children: Method and some preliminary findings. *Journal of Experimental Child Psychology, 3,* 333–342.

Goffman, E. (1967). *Interaction ritual.* New York: Anchor.

Goffman, E. (1974). *Frame analysis.* New York: Harper & Row.

Goffman, E. (1981). *Forms of talk.* Philadelphia: University of Pennsylvania Press.

Goodluck, H. (1991). *Language acquisition.* Oxford, England: Blackwell.

Goodwin, C. (1981). *Conversational organization. Interaction between speakers and hearers.* New York: Academic.

Graumann, C., & Hermann, T. (1988). Other-relatedness in language processing. *Journal of Language and Social Psychology, 7,* 159–168.

Gruber, H., & Voneche, J. (Eds.). (1977). *The essential Piaget.* New York: Basic Books.

Gumperz, J. (1982a). *Discourse strategies.* Cambridge, England: Cambridge University Press.

Gumperz, J. (1982b). *Language and social identity.* Cambridge, England: Cambridge University Press.

Hall, J. (1993). The role of oral practices in the accomplishment of our everyday lives: The sociocultural dimension of interaction with implications for the learning of another language. *Applied Linguistics, 14,* 145–166.

Hall, J. (1995). (Re)creating our worlds with words: A sociolinguistic perspective of face-to-face interaction. *Applied Linguistics, 16,* 206–232.

Hatch, E. (Ed.). (1978a). *Second language acquisition. A book of readings.* Rowley, MA: Newbury House.

Hatch, E. (1978b). Discourse analysis and second language acquisition. In E. Hatch (Ed.), *Second language acquisition. A book of readings* (pp. 401–435). Rowley, MA: Newbury House.

Hatch, E. (1983). Simplified input and second language acquisition. In R. Andersen (Ed.), *Pidginization and creolization as language acquisition* (pp. 18–31). Rowley, MA: Newbury House.

Hatch, E., & Lazaraton, A. (1991). *The research manual: Design and statistics for applied linguistics.* New York: Newbury House.

Hawkins, B. (1985). Is an "appropriate response" always so appropriate? In S. Gass & C. Madden (Eds.), *Input in second language acquisition* (pp. 162–178). Rowley, MA: Newbury HOuse.

Heritage, J. (1984). *Garfinkel and ethnomethodology.* Cambridge, England: Polity Press.

Higgins, E. (1992). Achieving "shared reality" in the communication game: A social action that creates meaning. *Journal of Language and Social Psychology, 11,* 107–131.

Higgins, E., Fondocaro, R., & McCann, C. (1981). Rules and roles: The "Communication Game" and speaker–listener processes. In W. Dickson (Ed.), *Children's oral communication skills* (pp. 289–312). New York: Academic.

Hill, L. (1960). *Picture composition book.* London: Longman.

Hinds, J. (1987). Reader versus writer responsibility. In U. Connor & R. Kaplan (Eds.), *Writing across languages: Analysis of L2 text* (pp. 87–98). Reading, MA: Addison-Wesley.

Hubbell, R. (1981). *Children's language disorders. An integrated approach.* Englewood Cliffs, NJ: Prentice-Hall.

Hudson, T. (1993). Nothing does not equal zero. Problems with applying developmental sequence findings to assessment and pedagogy. *Studies in Second Language Acquisition, 15,* 461–493.

Huebner, T. (1983). *A longitudinal analysis of the acquisition of English.* Ann Arbor, MI: Karoma.

Huebner, T. (1989). Establishing point of view: The development of coding mechanisms in a second language for the expression of cognitive and perceptual organization. *Linguistics, 27,* 111–143.

Hulstijn, J. (1989). A cognitive view on interlanguage variability. In M. Eisenstein (Ed.), *The dynamic interlanguage. Empirical studies in second language variation* (pp. 17–31). New York: Plenum.

Hulstijn, J., & Hulstijn, W. (1984). Grammatical errors as a function of processing constraints and explicit knowledge. *Language Learning, 34,* 23–43.

Husserl, E. (1978). *Formal and transcendental logic* (D. Cairns, Trans.). The Hague, Netherlands: Martinus Nijhoff. (Original work published 1929)

Hyltenstam, K. (1992). Non-native features of near-native speakers: On the ultimate attainment of childhood L2 learners. In R. J. Harris (Ed.), *Cognitive processing in bilinguals.* (pp. 351–368). Amsterdam: Elsevier.

Hymes, D. (1971). *On communicative competence.* Philadelphia: University of Pennsylvania Press.

Hymes, D. (1972). On communicative competence. In J. Pride & J. Holmes (Eds.), *Sociolinguistics* (pp. 269–293). Harmondsworth, Middlesex, England: Penguin.

Hymes, D. (1974). *Foundations in sociolinguistics.* Philadelphia: University of Pennsylvania Press.

Ingram, D. (1989). *First language acquisition.* Cambridge, England: Cambridge University Press.

Ironsmith, M., & Whitehurst, G. (1978a). The development of listener abilities in communication: How children deal with ambiguous information. *Child Development, 49,* 348–352.

Ironsmith, M., & Whitehurst, G. (1978b). How children learn to listen: The effects of modelling feedback styles on children's performance in referential communication. *Developmental Psychology, 14,* 546–554.

Isaacs, E., & Clark, H. (1987). References in conversation between experts and novices. *Journal of Experimental Psychology, 116,* 26–37.

Jackson, S., & Jacobs, S. (1982). Ambiguity and implicature in children's discourse comprehension. *Journal of Child Language, 9*, 209–216.

Jamieson, J. (1994). Instructional discourse strategies: Differences between hearing and deaf mothers of deaf children. *First Language, 14*, 153–171.

Jamieson, J., & Pedersen, E. (1993). Deafness and mother-child interaction: scaffolded instruction and the learning of problem-solving skills. *Early Development and Parenting, 2*, 229–242.

Jewson, J., Sachs, J., & Rohner, R. (1981). The effect of a narrative context on the verbal style of middle-class and lower-class children. *Language in Society, 10*, 201–215.

Johnson, D. (1992). *Approaches to research in second language learning.* New York: Longman.

Johnson, J., & Newport, E. (1989). Critical period effects in second language learning: The influence of maturational state on the acquisition of English as a second language. *Cognitive Psychology, 21*, 60–99.

Johnson, K. (1981). Writing. In K. Johnson & K. Morrow (Eds.), *Communication in the classroom* (pp. 93–107). London: Longman.

Jorden, E. (1992). Culture in the Japanese classroom: A pedagogical paradox. In C. Kramsch & S. McConnell-Ginet (Eds.), *Text and context* (pp. 156–167). Lexington, MA: Heath.

Karmiloff-Smith, A. (1986). Some fundamental aspects of language development after age 5. In P. Fletcher & M. Garman (Eds.) *Language acquisition. Studies in first language development* (pp. 455–474). Cambridge, England: Cambridge University Press.

Kasper, G. (Ed.). (1995). *Pragmatics of Chinese as native and target language.* University of Hawaii: Second Language Teaching and Curriculum Center.

Kasper, G., & Blum-Kulka, S. (Eds.). (1993). *Interlanguage pragmatics.* Oxford, England: Oxford University Press.

Kasper, G., & Kellerman, E. (Eds.) (1997). *Communication strategy research: Psycholinguistic and sociolinguistic aspects.* London: Longman.

Kellerman, E. (1991). Compensatory strategies in second language research: A critique, a revision, and some (non-) implications for the classroom. In R. Phillipson, E. Kellerman, L. Selinker, M. Sharwood Smith, & M. Swain (Eds.), *Foreign/second language pedagogy research* (pp. 142–161). Clevedon, England: Multilingual Matters.

Kellerman, E., Ammerlaan, T., Bongaerts, T., & Poulisse, N. (1990). System and hierarchy in L2 compensatory strategies. In R. Scarcella, E. Andersen, & S. Krashen (Eds.), *Developing communicative competence in a second language* (pp. 163–178), New York: Newbury House.

Kellerman, E., & Bialystok, E. (1997). On psychological plausibility in the study of communication strategies. In G. Kasper & E. Kellerman (Eds.), *Communication strategy research: Psycholinguistic and sociolinguistic aspects.* London: Longman.

Kellerman, E., Bongaerts, T., & Poulisse, N. (1987). Strategy and system in L2 referential communication. In R. Ellis (Ed.), *Second language acquisition in context* (pp. 100–112) Englewood Cliffs, NJ: Prentice-Hall.

King, S. (Ed.). (1989). *Human communication as a field of study: Selected contemporary views.* Albany, NY: SUNY Press.

Krashen, S. (1981). *Second language acquisition and second language learning.* Oxford, England: Pergamon.

Krashen, S. (1982). *Principles and practice in second language acquisition.* Oxford, England: Pergamon.

Krashen, S. (1985). *The input hypothesis: Issues and implications.* London: Longman.

Krashen, S., & Terrell, T. (1983). *The natural approach: Language acquisition in the classroom.* Oxford, England: Pergamon.

Krauss, R. (1987). The role of the listener: Addressee influences on message formulation. *Journal of Language and Social Psychology, 6,* 81–98.

Krauss, R., & Bricker, P. (1967). Effects of transmission delay and access delay on the efficiency of verbal communication. *Journal of the Acoustical Society of America, 41,* 286–292.

Krauss, R., & Fussell, S. (1988). Other-relatedness in language processing: Discussion and comments. *Journal of Language and Social Psychology, 7,* 263–279.

Krauss, R., & Fussell, S. (1990). Mutual knowledge and communicative effectiveness. In J. Galegher, R. Kraut, & C. Egido (Eds.), *Intellectual teamwork* (pp. 111–145). Hillsdale, NJ: Lawrence Erlbaum Associates.

Krauss, R., & Glucksberg, S. (1969). The development of communication: Competence as a function of age. *Child Development, 40,* 255–266.

Krauss, R., & Glucksberg, S. (1977). Social and nonsocial speech. *Scientific American, 236,* 100–105.

Krauss, R., & Rotter, G. (1968). Communication abilities of children as a function of status and age. *Merrill-Palmer Quarterly, 14,* 161–173.

Krauss, R., Vivekananthan, P., & Weinheimer, S. (1968). "Inner speech" and "external speech": Characteristics and communication effectiveness of socially and non-socially encoded messages. *Journal of Personality and Social Psychology, 9,* 295–300.

Krauss, R., & Weinheimer, S. (1964). Changes in reference phrases as a function of frequency of usage in social interaction. *Psychonomic Science, 1,* 113–114.

Krauss, R., & Weinheimer, S. (1966). Concurrent feedback, confirmation, and the encoding of referents in verbal communication. *Journal of Personality and Social Psychology, 4,* 343–346.

Krauss, R., & Weinheimer, S. (1967). Effect of referent similarity and communication mode on verbal encoding. *Journal of Verbal Learning and Verbal Behavior, 6,* 359–363.

Kraut, R., Lewis, S., & Swezey, L. (1982). Listener responsiveness and the coordination of conversation. *Journal of Personality and Social Psychology, 43,* 718–731.

Kumaravadivelu, B. (1991). Language learning tasks: Teacher intention and learner interpretation. *ELT Journal, 45,* 98–117.

Labarca, A., & Khanji, R. (1986) On communication strategies: Focus on interaction. *Studies in Second Language Acquisition, 8,* 68–79.

Lantolf, J., & Ahmed, M. (1989). Psycholinguistic perspectives on interlanguage variation: A Vygotskyan analysis. In S. Gass, C. Madden, D. Preston, & L. Selinker (Eds.), *Variation in second language acquisition: Vol. 2. Psycholinguistic issues* (pp. 93–108). Clevedon, England: Multilingual Matters.

Lantolf, J., & Appel, G. (1994). *Vygotskian approaches to second language research.* Norwood, NJ: Ablex.

Larsen-Freeman, D., & Long, M. (1991). *An introduction to second language acquisition research.* London: Longman.

Lefebvre-Pinard, M., Charbonneau, C., & Feider, H. (1982). Differential effectiveness of explicit verbal feedback on children's communication skills. *Journal of Experimental Child Psychology, 34,* 174–183.

Levin, I. (Ed.). (1986). *Stage and structure. Reopening the debate.* Norwood, NJ: Ablex.

Lightbown, P. (1987). Classroom language as input to second language acquisition. In C. Pfaff (Ed.), *First and second language aquisition processes* (pp. 169–187). Rowley, MA: Newbury House.

Lightbown, P., & Spada, N. (1990). Focus-on-form and corrective feedback in communicative language teaching: Effects on second language learning. *Studies in Second Language Acquisition, 12,* 429–448.

Lightbown, P., & Spada, N. (1993). *How languages are learned.* Oxford, England: Oxford University Press.

Linde, C., & Labov, W. (1975). Spatial networks as a site for the study of language and thought. *Language, 51,* 924–939.

Litowitz, B., & Novy, F. (1984). Expression of the part–whole semantic relation by 3- to 12-year old children. *Journal of Child Language, 11,* 159–178.

Lloyd, P. (1990). Children's communication. In R. Grieve & M. Hughes (Eds.), *Understanding children* (pp. 51–70) Oxford, England: Blackwell.

Lloyd, P. (1991). Strategies used to communicate route directions by telephone: A comparison of the performance of 7-year-olds, 10-year-olds and adults. *Journal of Child Language, 18,* 175–189.

Lloyd, P. (1992). The role of clarification requests in children's communication of route directions by telephone. *Discourse Processes, 15,* 357–374.

Lloyd, P. (1993). Referential communication as teaching: Adults tutoring their own and other children. *First Language, 13,* 339–357.

Lloyd, P. (1997). Developing the ability to evaluate verbal information: The relevance of referential communication research. In G. Kasper & E. Kellerman (Eds.), *Communication strategy research: Psycholinguistic and sociolinguistic aspects.* London: Longman.

Lloyd, P., & Beveridge, M. (1981). *Information and meaning in child communication.* London: Academic.

Lloyd, P., Boada, H., & Forns, M. (1992). New directions in referential communication research. *British Journal of Developmental Psychology, 10,* 385–403.

Lloyd, P., Camaioni, L., & Ercolani, P. (1995). Assessing referential communication skills in the primary school years: A comparative study. *British Journal of Developmental Psychology, 13,*13–29.

Lock, G. (1996). *Functional English grammar.* Cambridge, England: Cambridge University Press.

Loftus, E. (1979). *Eyewitness testimony.* Cambridge, MA: Harvard University Press.

Long, M. (1981). Input, interaction and second language acquisition. *Annals of the New York Academy of Sciences, 379,* 259–278.

Long, M. (1983a). Linguistic and conversational adjustments to non-native speakers. *Studies in Second Language Acquisition, 5,* 177–193.

Long, M. (1983b). Native speaker/non-native speaker conversation and the negotiation of comprehensible input. *Applied Linguistics, 4,* 126–141.

Long, M. (1983c). Native speaker/non-native speaker conversation in the second language classroom. In M. Clarke, & J. Handscombe (Eds.), *On TESOL '82* (pp. 207–225) Washington, DC: TESOL Inc.

Long, M. (1985). A role for instruction in second language acquisition: Task-based language teaching. In K. Hyltenstam & M. Pieneman (Eds.), *Modelling and assessing second language acquisition* (pp. 77–99). Clevedon, England: Multilingual Matters.

Long, M. (1989). Task, group, and task-group interactions. In S. Anivan (Ed.), *Language teaching methodology for the nineties* (pp. 31–50). Singapore: SEAMEO Regional Language Centre.

Long, M. (1990). Maturational constraints on language development. *Studies in Second Language Acquisition, 12,* 251–286.

Long, M. (1991). Focus on form: A design feature in language teaching methodology. In K. de Bot, R. Ginsberg, & C. Kramsch (Eds.), *Foreign language research in cross-cultural perspective* (pp. 39–52). Amsterdam: John Benjamins.

Long, M. (1993). Second language acquisition as a function of age: Research findings and methodological issues. In K. Hyltenstam & A. Viberg (Eds.), *Progression and regression in language* (pp. 196–221). Cambridge, England: Cambridge University Press.

Long, M. (1997). *Task-based language teaching.* Oxford, England: Blackwell.

Long, M., & Crookes, G. (1992). Three approaches to task based syllabus design. *TESOL Quarterly, 26,* 27–56.

Long, M., & Crookes, G. (1993). Units of analysis in syllabus design: The case for task. In G. Crookes & S. Gass (Eds.), *Tasks in a pedagogical context. Integrating theory and practice* (pp. 9–54). Clevedon, England: Multilingual Matters.

Long, M., & Porter, P. (1985). Group work, interlanguage talk, and second language acquisition. *TESOL Quarterly, 19,* 207–227.

Long, M., & Sato, C. (1984). Methodological issues in interlanguage studies: An interactionist perspective. In A. Davies, C. Criper, & A. Howatt (Eds.), *Interlanguage* (pp. 253–279). Edinburgh, Scotland: Edinburgh University Press.

Loschky, L., & Bley-Vroman, R. (1993). Grammar and task-based methodology. In G. Crookes & S. Gass (Eds.), *Tasks and language learning. Integrating theory and practice* (pp. 123–167). Clevedon, England: Multilingual Matters.

Lyons, J. (1977). *Semantics* (2 Vols.) Cambridge, England: Cambridge University Press.

Mackey, A. (1994). Targeting morpho-syntax in children's ESL: An empirical study of the use of interactive goal-based tasks. *Working Papers in Educational Linguistics (University of Pennsylvania), 10,* 67–89.

MacLure, M., & French, P. (1981). A comparison of talk at home and at school. In G. Wells (Ed.), *Learning through interaction. The study of language development* (pp. 205–239). Cambridge, England: Cambridge University Press.

Mangold, R., & Pobel, R. (1988). Informativeness and instrumentality in referential communication. *Journal of Language and Social Psychology, 7*, 181–191.

Maratsos, M. (1973). Nonegocentric communication abilities in preschool children. *Child Development, 44*, 697–700.

Markham, P. (1988). Gender and perceived expertness of the speaker as factors in ESL listening recall. *TESOL Quarterly, 22*, 397–406.

Markman, E. (1981). Comprehension monitoring. In W. Dickson (Ed.), *Children's oral communication skills* (pp. 61–84). New York: Academic.

Markman, E., & Gorin, L. (1981). Children's ability to adjust their standards for evaluating comprehension. *Journal of Educational Psychology, 73*, 320–325.

McTear, M. (1985) *Children's conversation.* Oxford, England: Blackwell.

McTear, M. (1987). Communication failure: A development perspective. In R. Reilly (Ed.), *Communication failure in dialogue and discourse* (pp. 35–47). Amsterdam: Elsevier.

Meline, T. (1986). Referential communication skills of learning disabled/language impaired children. *Applied Psycholinguistics, 7*, 129–140.

Messer, D., & Turner, G. (Eds.). (1993). *Critical influences on child language acquisition and development.* New York: St. Martin's Press.

Mitchell, P., & Russell, J. (1991). Children's judgements of whether slightly and grossly discrepant objects were intended by a speaker. *British Journal of Developmental Psychology, 9*, 271–279.

Moll, L. (Ed.). (1990). *Vygotsky and education: Implications and applications of sociohistorical psychology.* Cambridge, England: Cambridge University Press.

Morley, J. (1984). *Listening and language learning.* Orlando, FL: Harcourt, Brace, Jovanovich.

Neisser, U. (Ed.). (1987). *Concepts and conceptual development.* Cambridge, England: Cambridge University Press.

Newmeyer, F. (1991). Functional explanation in linguistics and the origin of language. *Language and Communication, 1/2*, 3–28.

Newton, J. (1995). Task-based interaction and incidental vocabulary learning: A case study. *Second Language Research, 11*, 159–177.

Noel, M. (1980). Referential communication abilities of learning disabled children. *Learning Disability Quarterly, 2*, 70–75.

Norman, D., & Bobrow, D. (1975). On data-limited and resource-limited processes. *Cognitive Psychology, 7*, 44–64.

Nichols, J. (1984). Functional theories of grammar. *Annual Review of Anthropology, 13*, 97–117.

Nunan, D. (1989). *Designing tasks for the communicative classroom.* Cambridge, England: Cambridge University Press.

Nunan, D. (1993). Task-based syllabus design: Selecting, grading and sequencing tasks. In G. Crookes & S. Gass (Eds.), *Tasks in a pedagogical context* (pp. 55–68). Clevedon, England: Multilingual Matters.

Nunberg, G. (1977). *The pragmatics of reference.* Bloomington: Indiana University Linguistics Club.

Ochs, E. (1982). Talking to children in Western Samoa. *Language in Society*, *11*, 77–104.

Ochs, E. (1987). Input: A socio-cultural perspective. In M. Hickman (Ed.), *Social and functional approaches to language and thought* (pp. 305–319). New York: Academic.

Ochs, E. (1988). *Culture and language development.* Cambridge, England: Cambridge University Press.

Olesky, W. (Ed.). (1989). *Contrastive pragmatics.* Amsterdam: John Benjamins.

Oliver, R. (1995). Negative feedback in child NS-NNS conversation. *Studies in Second Language Acquisition, 17*, 459–481.

Olson, D. (1970). Language and thought: Aspects of a cognitive theory of semantics. *Psychological Review, 77*, 257–273.

Omaggio, A. (1982). Using games and interactional activities for the development of functional proficiency in a second language. *Canadian Modern Language Review, 38*, 517–546.

Overstreet, M. & Yule, G. (1997). Locally contingent categorization. *Discourse processes, 23.*

Palmer, A., & Rodgers, T. (1983). Games in language teaching. *Language Teaching, 16*, 2–21.

Paribakht, T. (1985). Strategic competence and language proficiency. *Applied Linguistics, 6*, 132–146.

Pascual-Leone, J., & Smith, J. (1969). The encoding and decoding of symbols by children: A new experimental paradigm and a Neo-Piagetian model. *Journal of Experimental Child Psychology, 8*, 328–355.

Patterson, C., Cosgrove, J., & O'Brien, R. (1980). Nonverbal indicants of comprehension and noncomprehension in children. *Developmental Psychology, 16*, 38–48.

Patterson, C., & Kister, M. (1981). The development of listener skills for referential communication. In W. Dickson (Ed.), *Children's oral communication skills* (pp. 143–66). New York: Academic.

Patterson, C., Massad, C., & Cosgrove, J. (1978). Children's referential communication: Components of plans for effective listening. *Developmental Psychology, 14*, 401–406.

Patterson, C., & Roberts, R. (1982). Planning and the development of communication skills. *New Directions for Child Development, 18*, 29–46.

Pechman, T. (1989). Incremental speech production and referential overspecification. *Linguistics, 27*, 89–110.

Pechman, T., & Deutsch, W. (1982). The development of verbal and nonverbal devices for reference. *Journal of Experimental Child Psychology, 34*, 330–341.

Perdue, C. (Ed.). (1993). *Adult language acquisition: Cross-linguistic perspectives: Vol. 1. Field methods.* Cambridge, England: Cambridge University Press.

Peterson, C., Danner, E., & Flavell, J. (1972). Developmental changes in children's response to three indications of communication failure. *Child Development, 43*, 1463–1468.

Pfaff, C. (1987a). Functional approaches to interlanguage. In C. Pfaff (Ed.), *First and second language acquisition processes* (pp. 81–102). Rowley, MA: Newbury House.

Pfaff, C. (Ed.). (1987b). *First and second language acquisition processes*. Rowley, MA: Newbury House.

Piaget, J. (1951). *Play, dreams and imitation in childhood*. London: Heinemann.

Piaget, J. (1959). *The language and thought of the child*. London: Routledge & Kegan Paul.

Piaget, J., & Inhelder, B. (1956). *The child's conception of space*. London: Routledge & Kegan Paul.

Pica, T. (1987). Second language acquisition, social interaction, and the classroom. *Applied Linguistics, 8*, 3–21.

Pica, T. (1988). Interlanguage adjustments as an outcome of NS-NNS negotiated interaction. *Language Learning, 38*, 45–73.

Pica, T. (1991). Classroom interaction, participation, and comprehension: Redefining relationships. *System, 19*, 437–452.

Pica, T. (1992). The textual outcomes of native speaker–nonnative speaker negotiation. In C. Kramsch & S. McConnell-Ginet (Eds.), *Text and context* (pp. 198–237). Lexington, MA: Heath.

Pica, T. (1994). Research on negotiation: What does it reveal about second-language learning conditions, processes, and outcomes? *Language Learning, 44*, 493–527.

Pica, T., & Doughty, C. (1985a). Input and interaction in the communicative language classroom: A comparison of teacher-fronted and group activities. In S. Gass & C. Madden (Eds.), *Input in second language acquisition* (pp. 115–132). Rowley, MA: Newbury House.

Pica, T., & Doughty, C. (1985b). The role of group work in classroom second language acquisition. *Studies in Second Language Acquisition, 7*, 233–248.

Pica, T., & Doughty, C. (1988). Variations in classroom interaction as a function of participation pattern and task. In J. Fine (Ed.), *Second language discourse* (pp. 41–55). Norwood, NJ: Ablex.

Pica, T., Holliday, L., Lewis, N., & Morgenthaler, L. (1989). Comprehensible output as a result of linguistic demands on the learner. *Studies in Second Language Acquisition, 11*, 63–90.

Pica, T., Holliday, L., Lewis, N., Berducci, D., & Newman, J. (1991). Second language learning through interaction: What role does gender play? *Studies in Second Language Acquisition, 31*, 343–376.

Pica, T., Kanagy, R., & Falodun, J. (1993). Choosing and using communication tasks for second language instruction. In G. Crookes & S. Gass (Eds.), *Tasks and language learning* (pp. 9–34). Clevedon, England: Multilingual Matters.

Pica, T., Lincoln-Porter, F., Paninos, D., & Linnell, J. (1996). Language learners' interaction: How does it address the input, output, and feedback needs of L2 learners? *TESOL Quarterly, 30*, 59–84.

Pica, T., Young, R., & Doughty, C. (1987). The impact of interaction on comprehension. *TESOL Quarterly, 21*, 737–758.

Pienemann, M. (1985). Learnability and syllabus construction. In K. Hyltenstam & M. Pienemann (Eds.), *Modelling and assessing second language acquisition* (pp. 23–76). Clevedon, England: Multilingual Matters.

Pienemann, M. (1987). Psychological constraints on the teachability of languages. In C. Pfaff (Ed.), *First and second language acquisition processes* (pp. 143–168). Rowley, MA: Newbury House.

Pienemann, M. (1989). Is language teachable? Psycholinguistic experiments and hypotheses. *Applied Linguistics, 10*, 52–79.

Pienemann, M., & Johnston, M. (1987). Factors influencing the development of language proficiency. In D. Nunan (Ed.), *Applying second language acquisition research* (pp. 45–141). Adelaide, Australia: National Curriculum Resource Centre.

Pienemann, M., Johnston, M., & Brindley, G. (1988). Constructing an acquisition-based procedure for second language assessment. *Studies in Second Language Acquisition, 10*, 217–243.

Plough, I., & Gass, S. (1993). Interlocutor and task familiarity: Effects on interactional structure. In G. Crookes & S. Gass (Eds.), *Tasks and language learning. Integrating theory and practice* (pp. 35–56). Clevedon, England: Multilingual Maters.

Porter, P. (1986). How learners talk to each other: Input and interaction in task-centered discussions. In R. Day (Ed.), *Talking to learn: Conversation in second language acquisition* (pp. 200–222). Rowley, MA: Newbury House.

Poulisse, N. (1987). Problems and solutions in the classification of compensatory strategies. *Second Language Research, 3*, 141–153.

Poulisse, N. (1990). *The use of compensatory strategies by Dutch learners of English*. Dordrecht, Netherlands: Foris Publications.

Poulisse, N. (1997). Compensatory strategies and the principles of clarity and economy. In G. Kasper & E. Kellerman (Eds.), *Communication strategy research: Psycholinguistic and sociolinguistic aspects*. London: Longman.

Poulisse, N., & Bongaerts, T. (1994). First language use in second language production. *Applied Linguistics, 15*, 36–57.

Poulisse, N., Bongaerts, T., & Kellerman, E. (1984). On the use of compensatory strategies in second language performance. *Interlanguage Studies Bulletin, 8*, 70–105.

Poulisse, N., Bongaerts, T., & Kellerman, E. (1987). The use of retrospective verbal reports in the analysis of compensatory strategies. In C. Faerch & G. Kasper (Eds.) *Introspection in second language research* (pp. 213–229). Clevedon, England: Multilingual Matters.

Poulisse, N., & Schils, E. (1989). The influence of task- and proficiency-related factors on the use of compensatory strategies: A quantitative analysis. *Language Learning, 39*, 15–48.

Prabhu, N. (1987). *Second language pedagogy*. Oxford, England: Oxford University Press.

Preston, D. (1989). *Sociolinguistics and second language acquisition*. Oxford, England: Blackwell.

Psathas, G. (1995). *Conversation analysis. The study of talk in interaction*. Thousand Oaks, CA: Sage.

Rampton, B. (1997). A sociolinguistic perspective on L2 communication strategies. In G. Kasper & E. Kellerman (Eds.), *Communication strategy research: Psycholinguistic and sociolinguistic aspects*. London: Longman.

Ratner, E., & Rice, F. (1963). The effect of the listener on the speaking interaction. *The Psychological Record, 13,* 265–268.

Reeder, K., Shapiro, J., Watson, R., & Goelman, H. (Eds.). (1996). *Literate apprenticeships: The emergence of language and literacy in the pre-school years.* Norwood, NJ: Ablex.

Ricard, R., & Snow, C. (1990). Language use in and out of context. *Journal of Applied Developmental Psychology, 11,* 251–266.

Richards, J., & Schmidt, R. (Eds.). (1985). *Language and communication.* London: Longman.

Riesbeck, C. (1980). "You can't miss it!": Judging the clarity of directions. *Cognitive Science, 4,* 285–303.

Rinck, M., Williams, P., Bower, G., & Becker, E. (1996). Spatial situation models and narrative understanding: Some generalizations and extensions. *Discourse Processes, 21,* 23–55.

Rinvolucri, M. (1984). *Grammar games.* Cambridge, England: Cambridge University Press.

Roberts, L. (1993). *How reference works.* Albany, NY: SUNY Press.

Roberts, R., & Patterson, C. (1983). Perspective taking and referential communication: The question of correspondence reconsidered. *Child Development, 54,* 1005–1014.

Robinson, E. (1981). The child's understanding of inadequate messages and communication failure: A problem of ignorance or egocentrism? In W. Dickson (Ed.), *Children's oral cummunication skills* (pp. 167–188). New York: Academic.

Robinson, E. (1994). What people say, what they think, and what is really the case: Children's understanding of utterances as sources of knowledge. In C. Lewis & P. Mitchell (Eds.), *Children's early understanding of mind* (pp. 355–381). Hillsdale, NJ: Lawrence Erlbaum Associates.

Robinson, E., & Robinson, W. (1976). The young child's understanding of communication. *Developmental Psychology, 12,* 328–333.

Robinson, E., & Robinson, W. (1977). The young child's explanations of communication failure: A reinterpretation of results. *Perceptual and Motor Skills, 44,* 363–366.

Robinson, E., & Robinson, W. (1981). Ways of reacting to communication failure in relation to the development of the child's understanding about verbal communication. *European Journal of Social Psychology, 11,* 189–208.

Robinson, E., & Robinson, W. (1982). Knowing when you don't know enough: Children's judgments about ambiguous information. *Cognition, 12,* 267–280.

Robinson, E., & Robinson, W. (1983). Children's uncertainty about the interpretation of ambiguous messages. *Journal of Experimental Child Psychology, 36,* 81–96.

Robinson, E., & Whittaker, S. (1986). Learning about verbal referential communication in the early school years. In K. Durkin (Ed.), *Language development in the school years* (pp. 155–171). London: Croom Helm.

Robinson, E., & Whittaker, S. (1987). Children's conceptions of relations between messages, meaning and reality. *British Journal of Developmental Psychology, 5,* 81–90.

Robinson, P. (1995). Task complexity and second language narrative discourse. *Language Learning, 45*, 99–140.

Rodino, A., & Snow, C. (1997). "Y ... no peudo decir mas nada": Distanced communication skills of Puerto Rican children. In G. Kasper & E. Kellerman (Eds.), *Communication strategy research: Psycholinguistic and sociolinguistic aspects*. London: Longman.

Rogoff, B., & Wertsch, J. (Eds.) (1984). *Children's learning in the "zone of proximal development"*. San Francisco: Jossey-Bass.

Rollet, G., & Tremblay, R. (1975). *Speaking and writing with comic strips*. Montreal, Canada: Centre Educatif et Culturel, Inc.

Romaine, S. (1984). *The language of children and adolescents*. Oxford, England: Blackwell.

Rommetveit, R. (1974). *On message structure*. London: John Wiley.

Rommetveit, R., & Blakar, R. (Eds.). (1979). *Studies of language, thought and verbal communication*. New York: Academic.

Rooks, G. (1981). *The non-stop discussion workbook*. Rowley, MA: Newbury House.

Rooks, G. (1983). *Can't stop talking. Discussion problems for advanced beginners and low intermediates*. Cambridge, MA: Newbury House.

Rosch, E. (1974) Linguistic relativity. In A. Silverstein (Ed.), *Human communication: Theoretical explorations* (pp. 95–121). Hillsdale, NJ: Lawrence Erlbaum Associates.

Rosch, E. (1977). Human categorization. In N. Warren (Ed.), *Advances in cross-cultural psychology, Vol. 1*. New York: Academic.

Rosch, E. (1983). Prototype classification and logical classification: The two systems. In E. Scholnick (Ed.), *New trends in conceptual representation: Challenges to Piaget's theory?* (pp. 73–86). Hillsdale, NJ: Lawrence Erlbaum Associates.

Rosch, E., & Lloyd, B. (Eds.). (1978). *Cognition and categorization*. Hillsdale, NJ: Lawrence Erlbaum Associates.

Rosch, E., & Mervis, C. (1975). Family resemblances: Studies in the internal structure of categories. *Cognitive Psychology, 8*, 382–439.

Rosenberg, S., & Cohen, B. (1966). Referential processes of speakers and listeners. *Psychological Review, 73*, 208–231.

Rost, M. (1990). *Listening in language learning*. London: Longman.

Rost, M., & Ross, S. (1991). Learner use of strategies in interaction: Typology and teachability. *Language Learning, 41*, 235–273.

Rubin, K. (1976). Social interaction and communicative egocentrism in preschoolers. *Journal of Genetic Psychology, 129*, 121–124.

Rulon, K., & McCreary, J. (1986). Negotiation of content: Teacher-fronted and small-group interaction. In R. Day (Ed.), *Talking to learn: Conversation in second language acquisition* (pp.182–199). Rowley, MA: Newbury House.

Russell, G. (1997). Preference and order in first and second language referential strategies. In G. Kasper & E. Kellerman (Eds.), *Communication strategy research: Psycholinguistic and sociolinguistic aspects*. London: Longman.

Sachs, J., & Devin, J. (1976). Young children's use of age-appropriate speech styles in social interaction and role-playing. *Journal of Child Language, 3*, 81–98.

Sacks, H. (1992). *Lectures on conversation* (2 Vols.). Oxford, England: Blackwell.

Samuda, V., & Rounds, P. (1993). Critical episodes: Reference points for analyzing a task in action. In G. Crookes & S. Gass (Eds.), *Tasks in a pedagogical context. Integrating theory and practice* (pp. 125–138). Clevedon, England: Multilingual Matters

Sato, C. (1990). Ethnic styles in classroom discourse. In R. Scarcella, E. Andersen, & S. Krashen (Eds.), *Developing communicative competence in a second language* (pp. 107–119). New York: Newbury House.

Scarcella, R., Andersen, E., & Krashen, S. (Eds.). (1990). *Developing communicative competence in a second language.* New York: Newbury House.

Scarcella, R., & Higa, C. (1981). Input, negotiation, and age differences in second language acquisition. *Language Learning, 31,* 409–437.

Schachter, J. (1990). On the issue of completeness in second language acquisition. *Second Language Research, 6,* 93–124.

Schegloff, E. (1992). Repair after next turn: The last structurally provided defense of intersubjectivity in conversation. *American Journal of Sociology, 97,* 1295–1345.

Schiffrin, D. (1987). *Discourse Markers.* Cambridge, England: Cambridge University Press.

Schiffrin, D. (1990). The principle of intersubjectivity in conversation and communication. *Semiotica, 80,* 121–151.

Schiffrin, D. (1994). *Approaches to discourse.* Oxford, England: Blackwell.

Schmidt, R. (1993). Consciousness, learning and interlanguage pragmatics. In G. Kasper & S. Blum-Kulka (Eds.), *Interlanguage pragmatics* (pp. 21–42). Oxford, England: Oxford University Press.

Schober, M. (1995). Speakers, addressees, and frames of reference: Whose effort is minimized in conversations about locations? *Discourse Processes, 20,* 219–247.

Schober, M., & Clark, H. (1989). Understanding by addressees and overhearers. *Cognitive Psychology, 21,* 211–232.

Scholfield, P. (1987). Communication strategies—the researcher outmanoeuvred? *Applied Linguistics, 8,* 219–232.

Schütz, A. (1962). *Collected papers:* (Vol. 1), Arvid Broderson, (Ed.). The Hague, Netherlands: Martinus Nijhoff.

Schütz, A., & Luckmann, T. (1977). *The structures of the life world.* (R. Zaner & H. Engelhardt, Trans.). Evanston, IL.: Northwestern University Press.

Scollon, R., & Scollon, S. (1995). *Intercultural communication.* Oxford, England: Blackwell.

Scovel, T. (1988). *A time to speak: A psycholinguistic enquiry into the critical period for human speech.* Rowley, MA: Newbury House.

Seliger, H., & Shohamy, E. (1989). *Second language research methods.* Oxford, England: Oxford University Press.

Shannon, C., & Weaver, W. (1949). *The mathematical theory of communication.* Urbana: University of Illinois Press.

Shantz, C. (1975). *The development of social cognition.* Chicago: University of Chicago Press.

Shantz, C. (1981). The role of role-taking in children's referential communication. In W. Dickson (Ed.), *Children's oral communication skills* (pp. 85–102). New York: Academic.

Shantz, C., & Wilson, K. (1972). Training communication skills in young children. *Child Development, 43*, 693–698.

Sharwood-Smith, M. (1994). *Second language learning*. London: Longman.

Shatz, M. (1983). Communication. In P. Mussen (Ed.), *Handbook of child psychology: Vol. 3* (4th ed., pp. 841–889). Chichester, England: John Wiley.

Shatz, M., & Gelman, R. (1973). The development of communication skills: Modifications in the speech of young children as a function of the listener. *Monographs of the society for research in child development, 38*.

Sheen, R. (1994). A critical analysis of the advocacy of the task-based syllabus. *TESOL Quarterly, 28*, 127–151.

Shortreed, I. (1993). Variation in foreigner talk input: The effects of task and proficiency. In G. Crookes & S. Gass (Eds.), *Tasks and language learning. Integrating theory and practice* (pp. 96–122). Clevedon, England: Multilingual Matters.

Simons, H., & Murphy, S. (1986). Spoken language strategies and reading acquisition. In J. Cook-Gumperz (Ed.), *The social construction of literacy* (pp. 185–206). Cambridge, England: Cambridge University Press.

Singer, J., & Flavell, J. (1981). Development of knowledge about communication: Children's evaluations of explicitly ambiguous messages. *Child Development, 52*, 1211–1215.

Skehan, P. (1996). A framework for the implementation of task-based instruction. *Applied Linguistics, 17*, 38–62.

Slobin, D. (Ed.) (1985). *The crosslinguistic study of language acquisition*. Hillsdale, NJ: Lawrence Erlbaum Associates.

Smith, M., & Hanson, K. (1992). *Sparc picture scenes*. East Moline, IL: LinguiSystems, Inc.

Snow, C. (1987). Beyond conversation: Second language learners' acquisition of description and explanation. In J. Lantolf & A. Labarca (Eds.), *Research in second language learning: Focus on the classroom* (pp. 3–16). Norwood, NJ: Ablex.

Sodian, B. (1988). Children's attribution of knowledge to the listener in a referential communication task. *Child Development, 59*, 378–385.

Sonnenschein, S. (1984). How feedback from a listener affects children's referential communication skills. *Developmental Psychology, 20*, 287–292.

Sonnenschein, S., & Whitehurst, G. (1984). Developing referential communication skills: The interaction of role-switching and difference rule training. *Journal of Experimental Child Psychology, 38*, 191–207.

Spekman, N. (1981). A study of the dyadic verbal communication abilities of learning disabled and normally achieving 4th and 5th grade boys. *Learning Disabilities Quarterly, 4*, 139–151.

Sperber, D., & Wilson, D. (1986). *Relevance. Communication and cognition*. Oxford, England: Blackwell.

Stenström, A. -B. (1994). *An introduction to spoken interaction*. London: Longman.

Stubbs, M. (1986a). Language development, lexical competence and nuclear vocabulary. In K. Durkin (Ed.), *Language development in the school years* (pp. 57–76). London: Croom Helm.

Stubbs, M. (1986b). A matter of prolonged fieldwork: Notes towards a modal grammar of English. *Applied Linguistics, 7*, 1–25.

Surian, L., & Job, R. (1987). Children's use of conversational rules in a referential communication task. *Journal of Psycholinguistic Research, 16*, 369–382.

Sutherland, P. (1992). *Cognitive development today*. London: Paul Chapman Publishing.

Swain, M. (1984). Large-scale communicative language testing: A case study. In S. Savignon & M. Berns (Eds.), *Initiatives in communicative language teaching* (pp. 185–201). Reading, MA: Addison-Wesley.

Swain, M. (1985). Communicative competence: Some roles of comprehensible input and comprehensible output in its development. In S. Gass & C. Madden (Eds.), *Input in second language acquisition* (pp. 235–253). Rowley, MA: Newbury House.

Swain, M. (1995). Three functions of output in second language learning. In G. Cook & B. Seidlhofer (Eds.), *Principle and practice in applied linguistics* (pp. 125–144) Oxford, England: Oxford University Press.

Takano, Y., & Noda, A. (1995). Interlanguage dissimilarity enhances the decline of thinking ability during foreign language processing. *Language Learning, 45*, 657–681.

Tannen, D. (1984). *Conversational style*. Norwood, NJ: Ablex.

Tannen, D. (1989). *Talking voices*. Cambridge, England: Cambridge University Press.

Tarone, E. (1977). Conscious communication strategies in interlanguage. In H. Brown, C. Yorio, & R. Crymes (Eds.), *On TESOL '77* (pp. 194–203). Washington, DC: TESOL Inc.

Tarone, E. (1980). Communication strategies, foreigner talk and repair in interlanguage. *Language Learning, 30*, 417–431.

Tarone, E. (1981). Some thoughts on the notion of communication strategy. *TESOL Quarterly, 15*, 285–295.

Tarone, E. (1984). Teaching strategic competence in the foreign language classroom. In S. Savignon & M. Berns (Eds.), *Initiatives in communicative language teaching* (pp. 127–136). Reading, MA: Addison-Wesley.

Tarone, E. (1986). "The arm of the chair is when you use for to write." Developing strategic competence in a second language. In P. Meara (Ed.), *Spoken language* (pp. 15–27). London: CILT.

Tarone, E. (1987). Methodologies for studying variability in second language acquisition. In R. Ellis (Ed.), *Second language acquisition in context* (pp. 35–46). Englewood Cliffs, NJ: Prentice-Hall.

Tarone, E. (1988). *Variation in interlanguage*. London: Edward Arnold.

Tarone, E. (1989). On chameleons and monitors. In M. Eisenstein (Ed.), *The dynamic interlanguage. Empirical studies in second language variation* (pp. 3–15). New York: Plenum.

Tarone, E., Gass, S., & Cohen, A. (Eds.) (1994). *Research methodology in second language acquisition*. Hillsdale, NJ: Lawrence Erlbaum Associates.

Tarone, G., & Yule, G. (1987). Communication strategies in east–west interactions. In L. Smith (Ed.), *Discourse across cultures. Strategies in world Englishes* (pp. 49–65). Hemel Hempstead, England: Prentice Hall International.

Tarone, E., & Yule, G. (1989). *Focus on the language learner.* Oxford, England: Oxford University Press.

Taylor, D. (1988). The meaning and use of the term "competence" in linguistics and applied linguistics. *Applied Linguistics, 9,* 148–168.

Taylor, T., & Cameron, D. (1987). *Analyzing conversation.* New York: Pergamon.

Temple, J., Wu, H.-F., & Snow, C. (1991). Papa pig just left for pigtown: Children's oral and written picture descriptions under varying instructions. *Discourse Processes, 14,* 469–495.

Thompson, S. (1991). On addressing functional explanation in linguistics. *Language and Communication, 1/2,* 93–96.

Thomsen, S. (1994). *Sparc revised.* East Moline, IL: LinguiSystems, Inc.

Tomlin, R. (1984). The treatment of foreground–background information in the on-line descriptive discourse of second language learners. *Studies in Second Language Acquisition, 6,* 115–142

Tomlin, R. (1990). Functionalism in second language acquisition. *Studies in Second Language Acquisition, 12,* 155–177.

Traxler, M., & Gernsbacher, M. (1995). Improving coherence in written communication. In M. Gernsbacher & T. Givón (Eds.), *Coherence in spontaneous text* (pp. 215–237). Amsterdam: John Benjamins.

Trévise, A. (1987). Toward an analysis of the (inter)language activity of referring to time in narratives. In C. Pfaff (Ed.), *First and second language acquisition processes* (pp. 225–251). Rowley, MA: Newbury House.

Tsui, A. (1994). *English conversation.* Oxford, England: Oxford University Press.

Turian, D., & Altenberg, E. (1991). Compensatory strategies of child first language attrition. In H. Seliger & R. Vago (Eds.), *First language attrition* (pp. 207–226). Cambridge, England: Cambridge University Press.

Underwood, M. (1989). *Teaching listening.* London: Longman.

Ur, P. (1981). *Discussions that work.* Cambridge, England: Cambridge University Press.

Ur, P. (1988). *Grammar practice activities.* Cambridge, England: Cambridge University Press.

van Lier, L. (1996). *Interaction in the language curriculum.* London: Longman.

Váradi, T. (1980). Strategies of target language learner communication: Message adjustment. *International Review of Applied Linguistics, 18,* 59–71.

Varonis, E., & Gass, S. (1985a). Miscommunication in native/nonnative conversation. *Language in Society, 14,* 327–343.

Varonis, E., & Gass, S. (1985b). Non-native/non-native conversations: A model for the negotiation of meaning. *Applied Linguistics, 6,* 71–90.

Véronique, D. (1990). Reference and discourse structure in the learning of French by adult Moroccans. In H. Dechert (Ed.), *Current trends in European second language acquisition research* (pp. 171–201). Clevedon, England: Multilingual Matters.

von Stutterheim, C., & Klein, W. (1989). Referential movement in descriptive and narrative discourse. In R. Dietrich & C. Graumann (Eds.), *Language processing in social context* (pp. 39–76). Amsterdam: Elsevier.

Vygotsky, L. (1962). *Thought and language.* Cambridge, MA: MIT Press.

Vygotsky, L. (1978). *Mind in society.* Cambridge, MA: Harvard University Press.

Wachtel, T. (1980). Pragmatic approximations. *Journal of Pragmatics, 4,* 201–211.

Wagner, J. (1983). Dann du tagen eineeeee—weisse Platte—An analysis of interlanguage communication in instructions. In C. Faerch & G. Kasper (Eds.), *Strategies in interlanguage communication* (pp. 159–174). London: Longman

Wagner, J., & Firth, A. (1997). Communication strategies at work. In G. Kasper & E. Kellerman (Eds.), *Communication strategy research: Psycholinguistic and sociolinguistic aspects.* London: Longman.

Wanner, E., & Gleitman, L. (Eds.). (1983). *Language acquisition. The state of the art.* Cambridge, England: Cambridge University Press.

Wells, G. (1985a). *Language at home and at school.* Cambridge, England: Cambridge University Press.

Wells, G. (1985b). *Language development in the pre-school years.* Cambridge, England: Cambridge University Press.

Wells, G. (1985c). Preschool literacy-related activities and success in school. In D. Olson, N. Torrance, & A. Hildyard (Eds.), *Literacy, language and learning. The nature and consequences of reading and writing* (pp. 229–255). Cambridge, England: Cambridge University Press.

Wells, G. (1986a). The language experience of five-year-old children at home and at school. In J. Cook-Gumperz (Ed.), *The social construction of literacy* (pp. 69–93). Cambridge, England: Cambridge University Press.

Wells, G. (1986b). *The meaning makers. Children learning language and using language to learn.* Portsmouth, NH: Heinemann.

Wertsch, J. (1985). *Vygotsky and the social formation of mind.* Cambridge, MA: Harvard University Press.

Wertsch, J. (Ed.). (1985). *Culture, communication, and cognition: Vygotskyan perspectives.* Cambridge, England: Cambridge University Press.

Wesche, M. (1994). Input and interaction in second language acquisition. In C. Gallaway & B. Richards (Eds.), *Input and interaction in language acquisition* (pp. 219–249). Cambridge, England: Cambridge University Press.

Whitehurst, G. (1976). The development of communication: Changes with age and modelling. *Child Development, 47,* 473–482.

Whitehurst, G., & Sonnenschein, S. (1978). The development of communication: Attribute variation leads to contrast failure. *Journal of Experimental Child Psychology, 25,* 454–490.

Whitehurst, G., & Sonnenschein, S. (1981). The development of informative messages in referential communication: Knowing when versus knowing how. In W. Dickson (Ed.), *Children's oral communication skills* (pp. 127–141). New York: Academic Press.

Widdowson, H. (1983). *Learning purpose and language use.* Oxford, England: Oxford University Press.

Wierzbicka, A. (1986). Precision in vagueness: The semantics of English approximations. *Journal of Pragmatics, 10*, 597–614.

Wierzbicka, A. (1991). *Cross-cultural pragmatics.* Berlin, Germany: Mouton de Gruyter.

Wilkes-Gibbs, D. (1995). Coherence in collaboration: Some examples from conversation. In M. Gernsbacher & T. Givón (Eds.), *Coherence in spontaneous text* (pp. 239–267). Amsterdam: John Benjamins.

Wilkes-Gibbs, D. (1997). Studying language use as collaboration. In G. Kasper & E. Kellerman (Eds.), *Communication strategy research: Psycholinguistic and sociolinguistic aspects.* London: Longman.

Wilkes-Gibbs, D., & Clark, H. (1992). Coordinating beliefs in conversation. *Journal of Memory and Language, 31*, 183–194.

Willems, G. (1987). Communication strategies and their significance in foreign language teaching. *System, 15*, 351–364.

Willing, K. (1992). *Talking it through: Clarification and problem-solving in professional work.* Sydney, Australia: Macquarrie University: National Centre for English Language Teaching and Research.

Woken, M., & Swales, J. (1989). Expertise and authority in native–nonnative conversations: The need for a variable account. In S. Gass, C. Madden, D. Preston, & L. Selinker (Eds.), *Variation in second language acquisition: Vol. 1. Discourse and pragmatics* (pp. 211–227). Clevedon, England: Multilingual Matters.

Wolfson, N. (1989). *Perspectives: Sociolinguistics and TESOL.* New York: Newbury House.

Wolfson, N., & Judd, E. (Eds.). (1983). *Sociolinguistics and language acquisition.* New York: Newbury House.

Wood, D. (1988). *How children think and learn.* Oxford, England: Blackwell.

Wood, D., Bruner, J., & Ross, G. (1976). The role of tutoring in problem-solving. *Journal of Child Psychology and Psychiatry, 17*, 89–100.

Wood, D., McMahon, L., & Cranstoun, Y. (1980). *Working with under fives.* London: Grant McIntyre.

Wright, A. (1989). *Pictures for language learning.* Cambridge, England: Cambridge University Press.

Wright, P., & Hull, A. (1990). How people give verbal instructions. *Applied Cognitive Psychology, 4*, 153–174.

Young, R. (1984). Negotiation of outcome and negotiation of meaning in ESL classroom interaction. *TESOL Quarterly, 18*, 525–526.

Young, R. (1989). Input and interaction. *Annual Review of Applied Linguistics, 9*, 122–134.

Young, R., & Doughty, C. (1987). Negotiation in context: A review of research. In J. Lantolf & A. Labarca (Eds.), *Research in second language learning: Focus on the classroom* (pp. 212–223). Norwood, NJ: Ablex.

Yule, G. (1981). New, current and displaced entity reference. *Lingua, 55*, 41–52.

Yule, G. (1982). The objective assessment of aspects of spoken English. *World Language English, 1*, 193–199.

Yule, G. (1990a). Interactive conflict resolution in English. *World Englishes, 9*, 53–62.

Yule, G. (1990b). The spoken language. *Annual Review of Applied Linguistics*, *10*, 163–172.

Yule, G. (1991). Developing communicative effectiveness through the negotiated resolution of referential conflicts. *Linguistics and Education*, *3*, 31–45.

Yule, G. (1994). ITAs, interaction and communicative effectiveness. In C. Madden & C. Myers (Eds.), *Discourse and performance of international teaching assistants* (pp. 189–200). Alexandria, VA: TESOL.

Yule, G. (1996). *Pragmatics*. Oxford, England: Oxford University Press.

Yule, G., Anderson, A., & Brown, G. (1984). An objective approach to teaching and assessing talk. *Teaching English*, *17*, 12–19.

Yule, G., & Macdonald, D. (1990). Resolving referential conflicts in L2 interaction: The effect of proficiency and interactive role. *Language Learning*, *40*, 539–556.

Yule, G., & Powers, M. (1994). Investigating the communicative outcomes of task-based interaction. *System*, *22*, 81–91.

Yule, G., Powers, M., & Macdonald, D. (1992). The variable effects of some task-based learning procedures on L2 communicative effectiveness. *Language Learning*, *42*, 249–277.

Yule, G., & Tarone, E. (1990). Eliciting the performance of strategic competence. In R. Scarcella, E. Andersen, & S. Krashen (Eds.), *Developing communicative competence in a second language* (pp. 179–194). New York: Newbury House.

Yule, G., & Tarone, E. (1991). The other side of the page: Integrating the study of communication strategies and negotiated input in second language acquisition. In R. Phillipson, E. Kellerman, L. Selinker, M. Sharwood Smith, & M. Swain (Eds.), *Foreign/second language pedagogy research* (pp. 162–171). Clevedon, England: Multilingual Matters.

Yule, G., & Tarone, E. (1997). Investigating communication strategies in L2 reference: Pros and cons. In G. Kasper & E. Kellerman (Eds.), *Communication strategy research: Psycholinguistic and sociolinguistic aspects*. London: Longman.

Zuengler, J. (1989a). Assessing an interaction-based paradigm: How accomodative should we be? In M. Eisenstein (Ed.), *The dynamic interlanguage. Empirical studies in second language variation* (pp. 49–67). New York: Plenum.

Zuengler, J. (1989b). Performance variation in NS–NNS interactions: Ethnolinguistic difference, or discourse domain? In S. Gass, C. Madden, A. Preston, & L. Selinker (Eds.), *Variation in second language acquisition: Vol. 1. Discourse and pragmatics* (pp. 228–244). Clevedon, England: Multilingual Matters.

Zuengler, J. (1993). Explaining NNS interactional behavior: The effect of conversational topic. In G. Kasper & S. Blum-Kulka (Eds.), *Interlanguage pragmatics* (pp. 184–195). Oxford, England: Oxford University Press.

Zurif, E. (1990). Language and the brain. In D. Osherson & H. Lasnik (Eds.), *Language. An invitation to cognitive science: Vol. 1* (pp. 177–198). Cambridge, MA: MIT Press.

Author Index

Subject Index

A

Abstract figures, 45–50, 72
Abstract relationships, 71
Achievement strategy, 80
Adjustments, 82, 87
Ambiguous message, 21–22
Analytic frameworks, 79–87
Analytic strategy, 80–81
Appeal for assistance, 80–81
Approximation, 80–81
Arrange the houses task, 62
Assembly tasks, 61–64
Avoidance, 80–81

B

Back to back, 74, 77
Baseline data, 31–32
Block-building tasks, 63
Borrowing, 80–81

C

Cartoon strip, 65–70
Circumlocution, 80–81, 84
Clarification request, 15, 82–84, 87
Closed task, 33, 35
Code strategy, 80–81
Code switching, 81
Cognitive processing, 24, 27, 80
Collaboration, 10–11, 18, 33
Communication, 12–16, 19
    distanced, 75
    failure, 23–24
    interpersonal, 13–15, 19, 29
    strategies, 42, 48, 79–81, 83, 85–86
Communicative competence, 3, 17
    effect, 3, 26
    outcome, 84–85
    responsibility, 8–9
    stress, 42

Compensatory strategy, 80
Comprehension check, 82
Concept identification, 49–50
Conceptual strategy, 80
Confirmation check, 82–83
Context, 7–8
Contextualized, 75
Contingent query, 83
Convergent, 33, 35

D

Decision-making task, 71–72
Decontextualized, 24, 29, 75
Describing, 38–51, 78
Dialogue condition, 76–77
Directions, 51–64
Distinctions, 32–34
Divergent, 33, 35
Drawing, 52–53, 78
Dynamic relationship, 65

E

Effective talk, 8, 26
Egocentric speech, 2
Expert–novice, 34, 64
Eye contact, 74
Eyewitness accounts, 65–66, 78

F

Face to face, 76–77
Familiarity, 34–35, 42, 79
Feedback, 3, 21–22, 76
Film, 70–71
First language (L1), 4, 20–28
Flow diagram, 60–61
Foreignizing, 80–81